THE FOUR FACES OF SALES

HOW TO BUILD

YOUR PERSONAL VALUE CURRENCY
IN THE EYES OF YOUR CUSTOMER

JOHN ORVOS

iUniverse LLC
Bloomington

THE FOUR FACES OF SALES

HOW TO BUILD YOUR PERSONAL VALUE CURRENCY IN THE EYES OF YOUR CUSTOMER

iUniverse books may be ordered through booksellers or by contacting:

iUniverse
1663 Liberty Drive
Bloomington, IN 47403
www.iuniverse.com
1-800-Authors (1-800-288-4677)

Because of the dynamic nature of the Internet, any web addresses or links contained in this book may have changed since publication and may no longer be valid. The views expressed in this work are solely those of the author and do not necessarily reflect the views of the publisher, and the publisher hereby disclaims any responsibility for them.

Any people depicted in stock imagery provided by Thinkstock are models, and such images are being used for illustrative purposes only.

Certain stock imagery © Thinkstock.

ISBN: 978-1-4917-0472-1 (sc)
ISBN: 978-1-4917-0474-5 (hc)
ISBN: 978-1-4917-0473-8 (e)

Library of Congress Control Number: 2013915301

Printed in the United States of America.

iUniverse rev. date: 9/26/2013

Contents

Introduction

SELLING A SERVICE or a product is about closing deals. If you don't close, you're not making any money for yourself or your company. As a sales professional, closing is your bread and butter. The thing is, closing won't happen without an approach that makes you stand out from the thundering herd of competition—an approach that will make you more valuable in the eyes of the customer.

While the basics of the sales process have been the subject of countless books, I've learned from more than twenty-five years of experience as a sales leader that some of the more subtle aspects of successful selling can elude even savvy salespeople.

If you are an experienced salesperson, you surely understand what actions to take during customer interactions. As you begin a sales effort, you know it's vital to conduct research to gain access to the potential customer. When you meet the customer, you know to ask questions to qualify the sale and understand the customer's needs. You also know how to present your product or service to satisfy those needs. As a seasoned sales professional, you may have been successful using traditional techniques that served you in the past but now seem to be losing their effectiveness. You're doing everything right, but you're still somehow getting into a rut for mysterious reasons. Your tried-and-true techniques are suddenly falling short. If you are seeing diminishing returns on your sales efforts, it's likely you've been relying on overused, and sometimes overly obvious, techniques that just don't build enough personal value with the customer.

**Using a new sales approach can make you more
successful by building what's known as *personal value
currency* in the eyes of the customer.**

Just what is personal value currency? It's the trust and credibility
you build with the customer. It's the way you prove to your customer
that you, personally, can be a valuable asset.

As a salesperson, you can amass personal value currency by
demonstrating your ability to stay aligned with your customer's
interests in solving a problem. This comes first, even over your
own desire to sell something. Therefore, personal value currency is
about being valued, since you are looking out for the customer's best
interests. If the customer wins, you win. It's that simple.

Now, it's easy to say, "Go out, do some research, identify a need,
build a relationship with the customer, and ride in on your white
horse to make everything better." In practice, it's hard to build
personal value currency. It's not about being well liked and taking
right actions. If it were, we'd all be star sellers. The most important
concept is getting the "when" right—taking the right actions at the
right time. To do that, you have to look at the sales process very
carefully. We will identify four key steps, or faces, of sales.

**The whole concept of this Four Faces approach is that
every action taken is to build your personal value
currency by looking after the customer's best
interests—not pushing a sale.**

The reason I call them "faces" is simple. It's the easiest way for
you as the seller to know how you should approach the customer
interaction. When you have a face, it represents a mind-set or way

of thinking that will best communicate with the customer based on his or her own mind-set at the time. Your face is how you think and act—which directly reflects the customer's mind-set and what the customer is thinking—and stays aligned with that thinking. You will move through four faces based on the customer's mind-set:

1. **Sleuth:** Before you make first contact, your customer is busy with multiple priorities and believes he or she is doing fine without you. You need to have a mind-set, or face, that creates a compelling reason for the customer to want to meet you. Start by playing the role of detective, identifying and gaining access to your target customer through selective research. The goal of the sleuth is to use your knowledge of industry trends, pressures on the company, and the relevant executive to create a compelling reason to meet and establish personal value currency on your first contact.

2. **Doctor:** During your initial meeting, customers are wondering if you really care about helping them or care more about your commission check. Therefore, they are carefully watching how you conduct this meeting and will get their defenses up if they hear self-serving facts and questions. You need to have a mind-set, or face, that provides value based on the way you handle the meeting. Using the research from the sleuth, you play the role of doctor to earn customers' trust and get them to open up and discuss their situation. Here's where you increase your personal value currency while uncovering privileged insight.

3. **Quarterback:** When it's time to present your solution, the customer's anxiety is lower because of your doctor meetings. Now he or she is actually looking forward to what you have to present. This is the time to have a mind-set, or face, that

challenges customers to see your solution is actually the best way to solve his or her problem. When you play the role of quarterback, you're demonstrating that you understand the customer's situation, and you challenge him or her to look at new ways to solve a problem using your solution. This is where you maximize your personal value currency.

4. **Hero:** After you offer your proposal, your customer's anxiety shoots way up, since he or she realizes it's time to make a decision. As customers contemplate and measure you against the alternatives, they think about the risks of choosing you. You need to have a mind-set, or face, that is a calming force to overcome any concerns and close the sale. During this final step of the sale, you spend that precious personal value currency you've been building up to heroically overcome all last-minute concerns and issues. You carry the customer through the end of the sale smoothly, with everyone feeling like a winner.

You'll learn more about these Four Faces of Sales and how they help you build your personal value currency as we move through this book.

First, though, a few words about how I got into sales may help you see where I'm coming from. In 1995, I started a small software company with three partners. We relied on selling to grow the business. We did quite well. As larger competitors took notice and swooped in to take a piece of our little pie, we continued to outmaneuver and outflank them, mostly because of our superior selling. We had a hundred employees before we sold the business to a public company in 2000 for the sum of $45 million.

I initiated the company's sales efforts and was responsible for hiring, managing, and training the entire sales team. I knew we were on to something when we always seemed to have the upper hand in competitive situations, while we really should have been shaking in our boots. I loved the thrill of the pursuit and working with my sales team to find creative ways to win, even if we had a weaker offering. This is what I excelled at in my sales profession—finding and closing business. I really found my groove working on the front lines with my sales team. Not only did I enjoy pursuing new business, I had success at coaching my team to find ways to break new accounts.

The concepts in this book are drawn from my success as a sales leader working in my software company, and from the years that followed. I distilled what I learned into what I call the *Four Faces of Sales*, and I've put those concepts into practice. The Four Faces concept has been taught, tested, and proven with thousands of sales professionals, coaches, and managers. Dozens of companies, including Fortune 500 organizations, have incorporated these methodologies into their sales strategies.

It's all about building your personal value currency by knowing "when" to take the right action at the right time.

Let's examine how traditional sales approaches are missing the "when" of selling and how the Four Faces of Sales can help.

First Contact

- *Traditional Approach:* When do you make the cold call?
- *As a Sleuth:* You find out just enough relevant intelligence to stimulate interest in an impact statement. You advance to the

next face and set a meeting when you have provoked curiosity on the part of the customer.

Initial Meeting

- *Traditional Approach:* When do you present your solution?
- *As a Doctor:* You leverage your sleuth research to ask questions that benefit the customer to express their opinions, thoughts, and views about their situation. You advance to the next face to present your solution when you've discovered and confirmed the customer's ideal solution to a qualified problem.

Presentation

- *Traditional Approach:* When do you ask for the business?
- *As a Quarterback:* You reference your doctor knowledge about the customer's vision to quickly engage him or her in solving the problem. You then challenge the customer by presenting a better vision that highlights your product or service strengths. You advance to the next face to ask for his or her business when the customer agrees your solution is a good fit.

Sale Closing

- *Traditional Approach:* When do you close the sale?
- *As a Hero:* You instill confidence so that the customer will accept your proposal. You close the sale after you demonstrate that you can handle any concerns or price objections.

**Alignment is about understanding
customer's mind-sets, meeting them where they
are, and moving them to where they need to go.**

As you're probably seeing, this book is different from the other sales books out there because it goes beyond giving you the typical "what to do" and "how to do it" kind of information. The right skill at the wrong time does not yield results any more than the wrong skill does. With that in mind, this book will explain the skills you will need, teach you how to execute those skills, and ensure that you know precisely when to use them. *The Four Faces of Sales* will help you create a positive, branded buying experience by taking the right actions at the right time. You will raise your personal value currency and, in doing so, differentiate yourself from the competition and win more business.

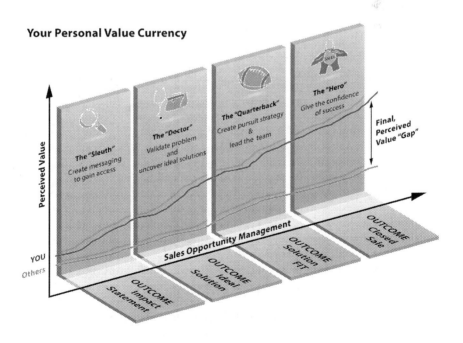

Julie's Dilemma

Julie, a dynamic salesperson, seemed to be getting close to signing a new account. Everything appeared to be going well … but then a problem arose. The sales process stalled at a critical time, right before the close. Fortunately, Julie had enough personal value currency to seal the deal. Before you learn how to make the Four Faces of Sales work for you, read this case study to see how it played out for Julie.

I was sitting at my desk at the busy software company I'd started with three partners, mulling over a thorny problem. Business was booming, and in my position as the vice president of sales and marketing, I was proud to be playing a pivotal role in making that happen. But on this particular day, I'd received some unpleasant and puzzling news. I leaned back in my chair and stared out the window at the gleaming skyscrapers of Manhattan. The rain and gloom of the day matched my mood.

I kept asking myself what I could have done differently to prevent a major deal from slipping away. It was the last day of the quarter, and there seemed to be little hope for turning things around. I envisioned what was sure to be a painful conversation with my CEO. And what was I going to tell my salesperson, Julie? Earlier that morning, she had knocked on my door with the bad news.

"They're not returning my calls," Julie said.

"What do you mean, they're not returning your calls? Who is not returning your calls?" I replied.

"Bob Glaser, Anne Worthington, all of them," Julie responded with a tone halfway between frustration and desperation. "For months, we've had very responsive communication with each other. Then I called Bob on Friday morning to confirm I was meeting him in the afternoon to get the order, and he didn't return my call. Anne is not responding either. I left them two more messages between Friday afternoon and yesterday and nothing," Julie added. "What do you suppose is going on?"

I knew all about Julie's sales opportunity. She had spent the better part of five months on this deal, one that represented more than a third of my quarterly forecast. We knew our competition had the deal in their crosshairs as well, but everything seemed to be lining up perfectly for another win. But now this? Why? After weeks of negotiation and open communication, just silence from the customer—a communication blackout.

None of it seemed to make any sense. After all, I had met Bob and Anne, the two key decision stakeholders, several times, and they'd told me that they preferred our solution over the competition's. I remembered their remarks about how "prepared, professional, and responsive" Julie had been throughout the many months of dialogue and meetings. As I reflected on what the customer said, it occurred to me that Julie had earned trust and credibility (personal value currency) in their eyes in a number of ways:

- Julie had cold-called and pointed out that the customer would become more operationally efficient by using a new technology. She created personal value currency with this initial call to gain access. She played the role of sleuth by uncovering an emerging problem and alerting the customer.
- She held a series of meetings to coauthor the customer's vision of improved productivity. She increased her personal value currency by the way she handled the customer during meetings. She played the role of doctor, asking questions to help the customer articulate thoughts on the current situation.

- Julie presented her solution, one that offered new perspectives and ideas on the best way to accomplish the customer's goal with our product. She overflowed her personal value currency based on how she listened and presented her solution in the context of what she heard. She played the role of quarterback by challenging the customer to think different.

There was one important phase of the Four Faces that was missing: the hero.

I knew what we had to do. This was the time to spend the personal value currency that Julie accumulated when she acted as sleuth, doctor, and quarterback. It was time to get in front of the customer and ask for the order.

"We're going in," I said.

Julie had a puzzled look on her face, but I knew she didn't have any better suggestions. Certainly, my decision to crash in on the customer unannounced could backfire. However, I had a hunch that our high trust and credibility levels made it worth the risk. I hoped this was like having money in the bank that Julie had deposited, in small amounts at a time, over the five months of working with the customer. I wasn't sure what to expect, but I believed it was time to make a bold move to see if all that Julie had earned would help close the sale.

By the time we made our way through midtown traffic to the main office of our customer—a sleek twenty-two-story building in Manhattan's financial district—the rain had stopped, but gray clouds were still thick in the noon sky. As we stepped off the nineteenth-floor elevators into the main reception area, I caught a glimpse of a meeting taking place just off to the left of the reception desk. And there was Bob Glaser, standing up, talking to a group of about eight executives. He didn't see us arrive, and my nerves kicked in. What would he think of us just showing up?

Just then, Bob turned and saw us sitting in the reception area. He motioned to the others that he was going to step out for a minute, came out of the conference room, and walked over to where we were sitting, a look of bewilderment on his face.

"Hi, Bob, it's good to see you," Julie said. "I brought my VP here to discuss your proposal."

"Julie and I thought we'd stop by to check on the status of your commitment to the solution we've proposed to you and to make sure there's nothing standing in the way of us working together," I added, shaking his hand.

"Come with me," was all Bob said.

With that, we were ushered into the conference room. Anne Worthington smiled and shook our hands, but everyone else was new to us. It was clear that despite Bob's invitation, the group only had a few minutes of time for such an unexpected interruption.

"We were actually just talking about some of the new technology we're bringing onboard. In fact, why don't you say hello to a few other folks on our executive team. You can help me assure them that we're making the right decision with your solution," Bob said. "You have five minutes."

Gulp.

I introduced Julie and myself, quickly recounted our shared five-month journey, and asked if the group believed our product was the best solution to their problem. Going around the room, the executives all had similar answers that our product was a good fit. However, when asked if they were ready to move forward with us, some had questions. One executive expressed a concern that a more established product (my competitor) had offered a better price for a similar solution. It was like finding gold to learn this.

I calmly responded to their questions for the next four minutes, in the end helping them to conclude that their concerns were nonissues. I wrapped up with about twenty seconds to spare, asking the executives if they were comfortable with my explanations and with working together. All nodded in the affirmative.

Bob actually signed the agreement in the reception area as we were on our way out. Crisis averted; normal breathing restored. We returned to the office having just closed a half-million-dollar deal. In doing so, we had bested some stronger competitors, and it was largely due to Julie's personal value currency. It was also due to our joint ability to show the customer that we could play the role of the hero, providing reassurance that our software was the best way to improve operations.

As we celebrated Julie's big win, I couldn't help but wonder about what went on. Why did the client fail to return Julie's calls and then take our word for it during our last five minutes of reassuring promises? It is common for clients not to return calls when they are considering the risks of making a decision and anxiety is high. They do this alone behind closed doors. But in Julie's case, she did have personal value currency. I pegged the lack of communication to customer anxiety, and I was glad we were able to overcome it by instilling confidence in the customer in those five minutes.

If Julie had not banked enough personal value currency in the eyes of the customer, we would simply not have been invited in when we showed up during the last stages of the sales pursuit. Even more, they certainly wouldn't have trusted what we said in our five-minute spiel enough to agree to a deal.

It became quite clear that we had to align with the customer's thinking and take the right action accordingly. In this case, Julie got close enough to the customer to relieve anxiety and calm everybody down sufficiently to make a decision in her favor. This was the hero face of the Four Faces of Sales approach. We were able to calm down the jittery customer and walk away with a favorable decision.

Customers inevitably have anxiety when it's time to make a decision, so they favor the salesperson they believe to be most credible and trustworthy. I concluded that we were successful in closing this sale because the customer believed Julie to be a credible and valuable resource. If Julie had not accumulated this positive reputation—this personal value currency—we would not have been given the floor with the executives, and they would have never believed all of the assurances of success we made to them.

It was this incident with Julie that inspired a true moment of understanding that the Four Faces of Sales was a strategy worth following and sharing with others. In part 1 of this book, you'll learn how to get started by putting on your sleuth face.

Part 1

The Sleuth Face

When you first call the customer, be a sleuth.

CHAPTER 1

Becoming Sherlock

IN "JULIE'S DILEMMA," we saw Julie overcome a common obstacle in sales. You uncover the customer's problem, present the product as a way to help the customer solve it, and then the customer gets cold feet. In Julie's case, it's important to ask why the executives allowed us to make that presentation to upper management. Julie's personal value currency played a major role in her success, but there is more to it than that.

Learning from Julie

Let's go back to the beginning. Remember, Julie had invested a great deal of time and energy on this deal. She had established herself as a credible, trustworthy source of information and help for these customers. She'd made many, many deposits into her personal-value bank account, and in the end, she needed to make a big withdrawal from those reserves to close the deal. Developing this personal value currency began with the very first call Julie made.

Most salespeople do not operate the way Julie did with this customer. Even Julie herself did not when she was newer to sales.

Polite beg calls get you nowhere.

We've all been there. You arrive at the office knowing that you're about to spend the day making cold calls. How many "no" answers will you receive? As usual, there were far too many to count yesterday. Today, you resolve, will be different. Today, you are going to get that yes and get yourself in the door. But as the day begins, you find yourself staring at the phone, which seems to weigh a thousand pounds. You resolve to push forward, because you must somehow find a way in. You aren't exactly sure how, but you know this is your job and this is what must be done.

I remember the countless days of calls we all made, Julie included. She made tons of calls, "dialing for dollars" as we called it. Using her nicest voice, she'd politely ask potential customers to meet with her, saying something like, "I will be in the area and was wondering if you would like to meet," or "I would like to meet with you to let you know about some of our new products," or "I was hoping we could meet to discuss your buying plans for next quarter." The approach didn't result in many meetings.

"When": Calling Too Soon

In retrospect, Julie was not really asking but rather hoping the customer would feel charitable and responsive to her "polite beg." She was making her calls too soon, before she had a compelling reason that would make the customer want to meet with her. In reality, this approach simply told target executives that she was not prepared. I'm sure they interpreted this to mean that if they met, they would be doing all the work to educate her, rather than the other way around.

Julie was essentially telling customers that she wanted to meet with them to benefit her, not the customer. Focusing on "polite beg calls" without having done adequate homework caused Julie to make a poor first impression and yielded few positive results. She failed to identify a compelling reason for the customer to meet with her. She was getting the "when" wrong by calling too soon.

> **Excelling in the initial call is about how to look out for the customer, not what the customer can do for you to sell him or her something.**

"When": Calling Too Late

Knowing she had to do research, there were times when Julie procrastinated too much before making the call. She knew that she needed to know about her target customer during her initial call, and she got caught up in thinking that more information was better too. Gathering a high pile of information would make sure she would always say the perfect thing.

Like so many of us, she had analysis paralysis. Perfection can be the enemy of progress. As Julie spent time planning, her call volume dropped, which in turn negatively impacted her pipeline.

I have seen many salespeople spend way too much time trying to get the perfect amount of information, and the sad thing is they don't *need* to be perfect. They only need to have enough information to create an idea or hypothesis about how they can help the customer solve a current or emerging problem. They need to play the part of the sleuth. Play a hunch and make the call!

Julie fell into a common trap. She let the cold calls intimidate her, causing her to do too much homework instead of taking action. This time, she was getting the "when" wrong by calling too late.

Your target customers endure a nonstop flood of calls from salespeople just like you. Customers are busy, and they often feel as if they are doing just fine. They cannot keep up with so many salespeople asking for their time. They may be thinking, *I am constantly getting calls from salespeople wanting to sell me something. Why should I spend time with another sales rep right now?*

My Moment of Clarity

For me, one call changed everything. I can still remember the VP's voice on the phone. He sounded interested. He was intrigued and wanted to learn more. He was not just appeasing me; his interest in meeting me was genuine. But why? What had I said differently this time? After careful analysis, I understood. I knew something new and different about what *he* cared about. I had almost dared him to meet me by making a more provocative call.

That was it! What worked in this case was to entice the customer, challenge him, and intrigue him by having something different to say based on something that I knew about his situation. This discovery put me on an all-new path. From that point on, I actually enjoyed making calls. I made them with purpose and confidence, knowing that I had something meaningful to say.

Cold calls are more effective if you identify a problem or a way to improve the customer's business and take it further by alerting someone who will care. If you get the right person curious, he or she will want to know more. Thus, I advised my sales team to call with the goal of "alert the relevant executive about a current or emerging problem that will stimulate curiosity and motivate them to meet you."

How did Julie take this theory and actually put it into practice? How did she create intrigue and entice the customer to meet her? It all began with her focus. Instead of concentrating her efforts on knowing everything about facts and figures, her new focus was all about doing research that would enable her to form a hypothesis about how a particular executive will deal with a looming situation. Her new goal was to pique the customer's curiosity by sharing her helpful ideas that would impact him or her personally. It required her to become a sleuth—the first of the Four Faces of Sales—to uncover ideas that would intrigue the customer.

This shift in focus makes for an initial branded experience that sounds good and feels right to the customer. As a result, you will begin to create personal value currency and get an appointment for a first meeting.

Your Personal Value Currency

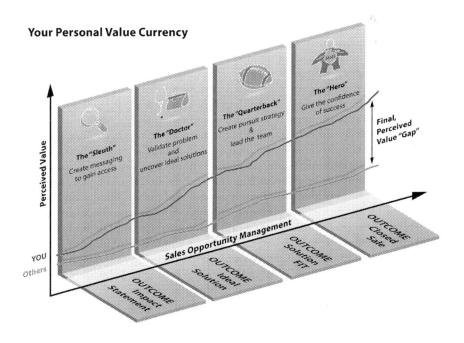

CHAPTER 2

Understanding ICE

WITHOUT PROPER RESEARCH before your initial call, you'll have nothing meaningful to say, and the customer won't feel there is value in meeting you. However, if you're not careful, you may waste your time looking for information that the customer doesn't care about. ICE enables you to find the right quality and quantity of information needed to stimulate the customer's curiosity and get you a meeting. ICE stands for the things you focus your research on:

1. **I**ndustry trends
2. **C**ompany pressures
3. **E**xecutive goals

The objective of your ICE research is to uncover information about a problem or situation that the person responsible might not even know. You will use this information to create an impact statement that identifies a problem or makes a suggestion for how to improve his or her situation. A call that makes the customer curious about an idea that you have to share will get you in the door. I'll go into the impact statement and the initial call later. For now, let's stay focused on the three components of ICE research.

Relative Impact on Sleuth research:

A pyramid labeled "Readily available research data on:" with three tiers — (E) Executive, (C) Company, (I) Industry — with arrows pointing to: Understand target Executive's personal drivers & Interests; Understand Company's business drivers and pressures/challenges; Understand Industy's top changes & trends

Industry Trends

Your ICE research begins with industry trends. When I say *industry*, I'm talking about large segments of the economy, such as automotive, finance, health care, consumer staples, and so on. However, it can also mean a grouping of people with similar interests—such as project managers, operations managers, and HR executives—that can represent a sort of mini-industry. Keep an open mind. Industry needn't be telecommunications. It could be CIOs from companies of all types.

By learning about the customer's industry, you'll gain invaluable knowledge that will feed into your company research (C) and executive research (E) later on.

Your sleuth research may begin with reading industry trade publications and attending events. However, it shouldn't end there. To succeed, you'll need to go a lot further by being a center of industry activity. By creating industry activities (I), you'll hear about what companies are out there doing (C). You will also develop goodwill with industry contacts that may help you with conducting executive research (E).

Creating Industry Activities

When you create industry activities, you brand yourself as a center of gravity. You become a point person who makes things happen and brings peers together on industry-related topics. How can you do this? Create ways for executives to hear what others in their position are thinking about topics of interest and give them opportunities to make connections. By making yourself a channel for this type of contact, you build your personal value currency. Two ways to do this are creating an industry LinkedIn group and hosting industry events.

LinkedIn

Executives within an industry are curious to know what others in their position are thinking about a particular topic. Satisfy their interest by creating a special industry group in LinkedIn (www. linkedin.com). Encourage members to post their own ideas and questions about trends, challenges, and successes. Ask group members to adhere to the rules of learning and sharing views on industry challenges, and creating new industry peer relationships. As the owner of this group, your name will be known to everyone.

It's simple to replicate your efforts to target multiple industries. For instance, if you sell software to all industries, you can start by creating LinkedIn groups for media, finance, telecommunications, and insurance. This is a lightweight way to bring people together on common topics.

Blogging would be an ideal way to establish credibility, but you likely don't have the time or expertise to do this. If this is the case, it is more practical and time-efficient to leverage other experts to blog on your behalf in your LinkedIn groups. That way, you are not responsible to keep up the content but only to include experts who can be leveraged in your LinkedIn group.

Industry Events

Your potential customers are interested in making connections with their industry peers. Capitalize on this by creating events and web conferences where peers can meet and discuss industry-related topics. This is different from typical networking events where participants are on their own to wander around and make connections. Instead, you make these connections for the attendees since your events are all about them.

Peer connections will emerge naturally, unforced, when you draw the audience into group discussions. For example, you might host a web conference on industry trends or moderate a panel at a forum event. When you are in front of the crowd, you are their connector to others.

Hosting Industry Events

By inviting (Sending out e-mails and calling) potential customers to a web conference or forum related on trends in their industry, you get in front of them outside the setting of a sales meeting. During your event, facilitate a high-tempo venue for participants to connect on topics of interest. Never let participants be responsible to network on their own or just show up, sit there and listen to a speaker drone on about a topic, and then leave. You have to make this fun if you want them to come back. You are responsible for make these introductions for them.

Running an executive forum isn't hard. Follow these steps:

1. Ask everyone in the room (or web conference) to give a ten-second introduction, including name, title, and company.

2. Have one participant (who you got to commit to doing this before the event) share a success story on a relevant topic. It's your job to join in several times to ask clarifying questions in front of the audience. This gives a feeling like it's a TV or radio talk show and you are the host, getting guests to talk more about what is on their mind. You are getting the audience involved and excited by rephrasing what each participant is saying.

3. Politely ask the participant to clarify by saying, "I am not sure the audience understands that point," or "The audience might find that part a bit confusing or hard to believe." When you do this, ask the audience to comment on your question and ask if they would like to add to it. This gets a conversation going around the room.

Never call on nonvolunteers, but rather say, "I see a few companies like yours in the audience that might have different perspectives on that." Like a talk-show host, you make it fun for the audience by getting the conversation going with your rephrasing and clarifying questions about what the participant is saying. Peer-to-peer networking naturally occurs on the topic of interest. The best part is, you are the center of making good feelings and connections occur while learning about industry-related trends.

Company Pressures

While conducting industry research is essential, the sleuth must also understand how the customer makes money and what pressures the company (C) must manage. These pressures may be coming from competitors, customers, finances, and operations, as well as compliance requirements. What new investments or initiatives are underway to deal with these pressures—such as a mergers, business investments, reorganization, product announcements, or technology initiatives?

Company Pressure Table

Your first step is to create a company pressure table in order to understand how company pressures affect how your customer makes money. You'll use what you have learned from industry (I) activities, as well as information the company releases as current news and events. Check Twitter (www.twitter.com) and the company's website. Companies use Twitter accounts to communicate news and events to followers. On the company's website, click under investor or media relations to find annual reports (public companies only), speeches from executives, and press releases.

Creating a company pressure table enhances your chances of identifying a problem or a method to improve the business that will get you your first meeting. Create a table that answers the following questions:

1. How do the company's competitive pressures impact how they make money?
    *   Who is the company's biggest competitor?
    *   How large of a threat does it pose?

- What is its market share?
- Is your target company exposed to new competitive threats from emerging niche competitors?
- Has any competitor developed a unique solution that would pose a competitive threat to this company?
- How does this company stay ahead of its competitors?
- What is the company's key competitive advantage?

2. How do the company's customer pressures impact how it makes money?
   - What is the company's current level of customer satisfaction?
   - Has that percentage been improving or declining over the past few years?
   - How are their customers' expectations changing? How are they striving to meet these expectations?

3. How do the company's financial pressures impact how they make money?
   - How does the financial performance of this company compare to similarly sized companies in the industry?
   - What is the direction of the company's revenue, profits, and costs?
   - What controls has the company put in place to address slumping profits and/or revenues and rising costs?
   - What are the major financial trends and metrics for similar-size companies in this industry?

4. How do the company's operational pressures impact how they make money?

- Does the company have the right skill mix in place to achieve its major objectives over the next three to five years?
- Has the company recently experienced substantial organizational changes?
- Have there been any major cultural changes within the organization as a result of mergers and acquisitions?

5. How do the company's compliance and regulatory pressures impact how they make money?
   - What regulatory issues is the company dealing with at the present time?
   - Is there any impending legislation that could result in new regulations that would affect this company (either positively or negatively)?
   - How will any of these regulatory issues impact the company's financials?
   - What new technology or other changes may have to be made to conform to these new regulations?

Executive Goals

You've enmeshed yourself in the customer's industry and charted out the many pressures the customer is facing. Next, select a company pressure and ask, "Who cares?" Who is the person charged with handling this particular company pressure? There is one high-level executive (E) who has the most to lose or gain because of this pressure. This person is the sleuth's target executive. This is the person you want to call when you've finished your ICE research.

Of course, the target executive is aware of the company pressure, may have taken steps to deal with the situation. Therefore, he or she is likely feeling just fine with the current efforts in place. As a sleuth, however, you know this is never true. It is your job to dig up something the executive does not know. Discover something more the executive can do about the current situation. There are always blind spots.

Blind spots occur when the target executives do not realize their situation may be different, larger, or trickier than first anticipated. They may have misread the size, speed, or duration of the situation they are facing. For example, an executive may believe something will be accomplished quickly, when in reality, it will take much longer and be more expensive and problematic.

By uncovering a problem and alerting the target executive, you will solidify your position. You are helping out by telling the executive something he or she doesn't know about a looming problem, and that executive will want to meet you.

Conducting ICE Research Calls

The ICE research call is designed to validate *industry* knowledge, confirm *company* pressures, and identify your target *executive* who is dealing with it and his or her blind spots. Make these ICE research calls to individuals in the lower and middle levels within the customer's organization. Think about ICE research calling as being "low and wide." You might call on executive assistants, department managers, customer service, and sales people. Even better is when you have an inbound lead. This in itself is a perfect person to make a sleuth call since he or she will be more inclined to speak with you.

If your company receives inbound leads or inquiries, you can use this as an opportunity to make ICE research calls to those individuals. Also, this is where people you met and built goodwill with during your industry activities can be very helpful.

Knowledge is power, so take the time to learn about a target industry (I) and company (C) before your research call.

Your ICE research calls will move through three steps: disarm, warm up, and request. I've provided a sample script for each of the steps to give you some pointers.

Disarm

Sample script: "Hi, I work with your company [or within your industry] and was hoping that you could point me in the right direction."

Strategy: By requesting advice and direction, you lower the informant's defenses and reduce any tension and suspicion that you are selling something. If you come in with "Can you please help me?" using a sleuth tone and approach, the person you're talking to is more likely to be helpful. When you make an ICE research call, your tone is respectful and friendly but never bubbly and enthusiastic, which can come across as fake.

Warm Up

Sample script: "In working within your industry, we are seeing trends from other companies like yours that improve their business."

Strategy: Once you get the person on the other end of the phone engaged and ready to help, you should share some of what you have learned about the industry. This is designed to demonstrate that you understand the person's industry based on your research. Be careful that your tone is not one of persuading your contact of your views. People can see your intent and will likely put up their defenses.

Request

Sample script: "I read that your CEO outlined a new goal to improve business this year due to emerging customer and competitive pressures. I'm wondering if you know anything more about these pressures? … Are there current initiatives underway addressing these pressures? … Could you point me to the area in your company that would be responsible for dealing with them? … Do you know who is in charge and what they are doing about it currently? … How are these initiatives going? … Is there anything they are missing or not addressing yet?"

Strategy: Here's where you get down to brass tacks. Your objective is twofold: you need to learn more about the company pressures, and you need to identify the target executive you'll eventually want to meet. Of course, these questions could set off alarms and raise defenses. So don't come on too strong. Assure the person that you're calling for research purposes only, because you're studying industry trends. That's the truth, and most people will want to share at least something about their company as it relates to the wider industry it serves.

Bear in mind that once you've got one industry down, you can apply what you've learned to multiple companies.

You know you've done enough ICE research when you have the intelligence to create an impact statement to stimulate curiosity. The time required might be a few clicks on web and ICE research calls over a few hours or a series of more involved meetings and calls. The goal is not to have a high quantity of information but rather the right quality to create your impact statement. Therefore, it usually takes less time, since you know you don't need to know everything about everything but rather have a goal that is specific to your target executive.

You are looking for micro assets of intelligence that apply to a particular target executive, not macro mountains of information. All you really need to create an impact statement is one intelligence nugget from I, C, and E—a general industry trend that contributes to a specific company pressure that a particular executive needs to handle. That's it. Once you have those three, you have enough to create a hypothesis, a hunch to why that executive would want to meet you. You have enough to create an impact statement.

You are done with ICE when you can move on to creating an impact statement using the intelligence you've gathered.

Your ICE research should have turned up a potential problem that your customer is facing as well as the target executive who cares. Your objective is to show you can help the target executive deal with it. Doing so immediately boosts your personal value currency, making you someone worth the executive's time.

Now it's time to move forward with the information you've unearthed. The next sleuth step is to craft what I call an *impact statement*, essentially a message conveyed via e-mail and then by phone that will get you in to see the target executive for a face-to-face meeting. The impact statement is all about sharing what you've discovered in a way that makes customers curious, convinces them that you know the industry and the company, and suggests that you are in a position to improve their business.

Using your newly acquired intelligence to come up with a hypothesis and carefully craft an impact statement will pay off by gaining access.

CHAPTER 3

Sleuth Hypothesis

THE SALES SLEUTH gathers information, and then he or she harnesses its power to generate curiosity and interest from the initial call. It's really not rocket science, but it is an approach that defies some of the tenets of traditional selling techniques. The beauty of the sleuth approach is that it gives you purpose from the start and helps to reduce the reluctance some salespeople have about cold-calling.

Your Impact Statement

An impact statement shares an observation and its ramifications to target customers. Your observation relates to their industry trends and company pressures. The ramifications of your hypothesis focus on how these observations affect the company's ability to make money and/or operate more efficiently, as well as why that individual executive should care. The impact statement will have a more powerful effect when you incorporate specific data and statistics—for example, a 20 percent improvement or $100,000 in savings. Here's an example of what I'm talking about:

> "In working within your industry and company, we have studied initiatives like yours in which other companies tried to improve their business. With a recent study indicating an 80 percent failure rate, we would like to discuss how you can avoid a few emerging pitfalls."

The pitfalls are the ramification. Most executives will be interested in avoiding an 80 percent failure rate. You've gotten the executive's attention at this point, which is what you want!

Always remember that the goal of an impact statement is to entice your target executive to be curious enough that he or she will want to spend precious time with you. You will need to grab the executives' attention, because they'll be thinking, *Why would I want to meet this salesperson?* To do so, you will play on their fears, using your provocative view and offering a fresh perspective that places their situation in a jarring new light. Play on the customer's fear of missing out on something big:

- "We have discovered two companies that are implementing operational improvement initiatives [observation] that improve customer service, allowing them to create new product revenue streams that can grow their business 30 percent [ramification]."
- "A VP like you at another company was recognized for implementing an operational improvement initiative [observation] that improved customer service and increased market share 20 percent [ramification]."

Alternatively, you can key into the executive's fear of failure:

- "We would like to alert you to three possible mistakes [observation] that may put an extra burden on staff, which can double the time it takes to roll out the operational improvement initiative [ramification]."
- "An operational problem we have uncovered [observation] may be costing you $100,000 per year [ramification]."

**The delivery of your impact statement
comes down to I-We-You.**

I-We-You

Let's take a close look at the most essential components of your impact statement, whether it's delivered via e-mail or over the phone. The key concept is what I call the *I-We-You* element:

1. The "I" is who you are.
2. The "We" is what your company does.
3. The "You" is why the executive needs what you do.

If you're on the phone, the statement shouldn't take more than about thirty seconds or so. Remember, your customers' are busy. If you ramble on longer, you risk turning off customers and making them feel you're wasting their time. That may force them to interrupt you and say they are not interested or even hang up on you—and remember your name and company to avoid taking your next call.

The I-We-You statement offers a fresh perspective that frames the customer's situation in a jarring new light. It is designed to be delivered from a position of power based on your gathered intelligence.

Contrary to popular belief, the purpose is not to advertise your company or tell the customer how great your product or service is. Your I-We-You impact statement's sole purpose is to provoke the customer to believe that there is a potential problem that he or she will care about, whether he or she knows it or not. You're doing him or her a favor by calling. It's easy to get motivated to call when you call from a position of power with a purpose, not to push your product.

Now that you've created your impact statement, it's time to move on to the next sleuth step: actually making the cold call. Because you did ICE your research, your call presents the idea that only you will know how to help in this situation. Believe me, it'll be fun compared to cold-calling based on a traditional sales model. This time, you'll have a solid foundation of information to work from—information that convinces customers they need to meet you about their most puzzling problems.

You're on your way to becoming the Sherlock Holmes of getting in the door to set that first meeting!

CHAPTER 4

Making the Call

ONCE YOU HAVE developed your provocative impact statement, consider it to be an asset, one that can be used anywhere, at any time: cold calls, warm calls, at events, or even on an elevator or in the hallway. Regardless of how and where you first engage with your target executive, you have one shot at making a succinct, provocative statement that motivates that individual to set a meeting. Follow the steps below when approaching your target executive to set up that all-important meeting.

E-mail Your Impact Statement

E-mail is a great way to get the provocative message of your impact statement in front of your target executive. The hardest part of this step may be getting that executive's e-mail address if you haven't had any previous contact. Fortunately, most companies use formats that are consistent for all employees. If you know that Jane Doe's e-mail is jane.doe@companyname.com, you can figure that the e-mail address for your target executive John Smith is likely to be john.smith@companyname.com. There are exceptions to this rule, since companies are getting smarter about this. Sometimes they include a middle initial of the person's name or a number in the e-mail address. But these are the exceptions, and this approach can help with most of your efforts.

Of course, you have to get the company's e-mail format in the first place. You may have already discovered the format when you made your ICE research calls. If not, try these tactics:

- Search the company's website for the e-mail address of press contacts, and that will likely give you the format.
- On the website, look for a section such as "employment," "news," or "contact us." You will likely find the e-mail address of someone who wants to receive inquiries about the company, and you can pick up the format from that.
- Call the company and tell the receptionist you would like to e-mail a salesperson. Ask who that contact is and his or her e-mail. Typically, when you ask for sales, receptionists will be happy to give out an e-mail address.

Once you've got the format and made your best reverse-engineered guess at what the executive's e-mail address might be, call the receptionist with a "just confirming" question. Ask with the attitude that you already know the target executive and his e-mail address, but you are "just confirming" that the address you have is correct. The receptionist will most likely correct you if you're wrong, since you sound like you know what you are talking about.

If you're trying to get the e-mail address for John Smith, for example, say, "I am supposed to e-mail John Smith some information. My records show that his e-mail address is john.smith@abccompany. com. I wanted to make sure that this is correct, since I didn't get a chance to ask him and I want to make sure this gets to him." Should you meet resistance, assure the receptionist, "I'm not asking for his e-mail, but can you just confirm that this sounds right?" Now, even if you are way off, you still come in with something the receptionist can react to.

An effective e-mail that includes an abbreviated impact statement will entice your target executive to click "reply" and accept your offer to meet.

I've included a sample e-mail below for your reference. Notice that it incorporates the impact statement in abbreviated form.

Subject: Your "new" initiative at your company

As an introduction, my name is [your name], and I am the account manager for [your company] providing tools and consulting.

In working with senior-level executives in [the executive's industry] and, studying their efforts, I've made some observations that relate to your new corporate initiative as stated by your president and CEO in the 2012 annual report:

"… We are committed to taking a **new view of our businesses**. That means we **will invest in the businesses that will deliver** the highest risk-adjusted **returns** for shareholders."

I'd like to share my observations as they relate to your current efforts. We've discovered an opportunity to improve your strategy and boost productivity 20 percent by including three missing elements.

Can we arrange a thirty-minute discussion on this perhaps?

Call the Customer

Now you're ready to follow up on the e-mail you sent to your target executive. Remember to stick with the I-We-You format when delivering your impact statement. I've included a sample I-We-You script to give an idea of how your message might go.

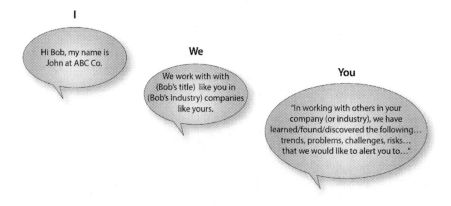

I (Who You Are)

"Hello, my name is John."

We (What Your Company Does)

"We are a solution provider specializing in the [customer's] industry. We work with companies or industries just like yours, such as ..." Say what *we* do for industries or companies like the one of your target executive. Share how your solution is benefiting those other companies. Show the executive that if he or she neglects to see you, the company will not enjoy the same benefits and solve similar problems.

You (Why the Executive Need to Meet You)

"I thought you would be interested in knowing that we have [observation] discovered a recent development that can double the costs of your current operational improvement efforts [ramification]." This makes it clear why "you"—the target executive—need to meet "I"—the very helpful person calling and e-mailing. This provokes and tempts the target executive to learn more about your observation and ramifications by setting a meeting.

Get the Customer Talking

Follow your impact statement with an open-ended question that gives the target executive a chance to respond. In the first twenty seconds, ask, "Are you interested in learning more?" Pausing to allow the target executive to speak will reduce the tension and allow the executive to gather his or her thoughts on the idea you shared in your impact statement.

It is here that you must resist the temptation to fill the silence with a long-winded story to be sure the target executive hears everything you have to say. This approach of letting the customer talk might go against your instincts, because you may be afraid that the target executive will simply say "I'm not interested" and hang up. On the contrary, if you do not give him or her a chance to speak and ramble on, you will be tuned out. The target executive will experience a drowning feeling and want to get off the phone (or move away from you) as quickly as possible.

Set a Meeting

Now, a lot has just happened in a very short period of time. The target executive will be thrown for a loop, since he or she has no idea how you know what you know. When you ask, "Are you interested?" the executive will be confused about how you came to form your idea or perspective and will naturally ask, "What do you mean? How do you know this?" This is exactly what you want to hear.

When the executive asks these questions, avoid the temptation to launch into a long speech about your company and products. Remember, the objective of your impact statement is to pique curiosity and provoke your target executive to set a meeting—not to reveal all the answers! In other words, make the executive say, "Huh?"

Startled readers might be thinking, *No! Don't give the customer an "out" to get off the phone!* This approach to an initial call may be frowned upon by traditional sales schools that say you need to talk your way in and don't let the customer off the hook until you get a meeting. But in this case, if you take the old approach of talking until he or she concedes a meeting, you might win the battle by keeping the executive on the phone a few minutes longer, but you will lose an opportunity to build your personal value currency. Rest assured, if you talk nonstop and never allow the executive to get a word in, he or she will not want to meet with you.

The core foundation of this calling approach is based on the sincere goal of trying to help your customer improve his or her situation or solve an emerging problem. It's not about out-talking the customer, because that depletes your personal value currency. The bet of this approach is that if you call from a position of power with a provocative impact statement, the customer will be curious enough to want to know more. Executives will also be surprised that you have the guts to respect their time and give them an out. If they do actually say they are not interested, that is still good, since you will use that objection as an opportunity to call again. Even if you lose this opportunity for a meeting, you win long-term return calls with new ideas, which builds your personal value currency.

It's okay if customers say no, though you hope they'll say yes and book a meeting.

In the traditional sales approach, we cringe when the customer wants to speak during our first call for fear of being rejected. In the sleuth approach, we welcome what the customer has to say. We are happy with any outcome, because we know that we are building personal value currency and are one step closer to gaining access and getting the meeting.

When customers ask questions, elaborate on the "You" and ask for the meeting again. The "You" tells them what's in it for them. This is all they really need to know (or really care about) when deciding if they should meet with you. After revisiting the "You," repeat your question, "Are you interested in learning more?" Keep doing this until they say "Yes." When your target executive gives the go-ahead, end the call to set a meeting with a statement like this:

"Based on your interest, I would like to set an initial exploratory discussion to share ideas. We understand your situation and will discuss ideas that are relevant to your goals. At the end of this meeting, you can make a decision as to whether there is value in proceeding. If you agree, can we arrange this, perhaps next week?"

Meeting booked!

Use Objections to Set a Meeting

After you have given your I-We-You impact statement and asked, "Are you interested?" the target executive won't always follow the script. Instead, he or she may have an objection to meeting. When the executive voices an objection, it is no problem. In fact, you can welcome these reservations and use what the executive says. Turn it around into a new reason to set a meeting. Here are examples of how to turn an objection into a reason to meet:

- *Your target executive says:* "I am not interested."
  You respond: "Okay. I am sure you have a good reason. Can I call you back when I have another idea?"
- *Your target executive says:* "We are doing this already" or "We have another vendor."
  You respond: "I can understand how you might think that. I have heard this from other companies that have not seen our solution and think they are already doing something similar. After we met once, they concluded that our solution was different from what they expected. In a thirty-minute

meeting, we can determine this as it relates to your situation as well. Can we set this?"

- *Your target executive says*: "You are too expensive."

  You respond: "Many of my customers reacted that way until I helped them discover the costs of not using our solution. We do a quick, painless cost/benefit analysis with our potential customers. All of them have payback quicker than the alternative you are using. In a thirty-minute meeting, I will be able to prove if our solution may, in fact, be less expensive as it relates to your situation. Can we set this?" While you're best advised not to talk price at this early stage, if the question comes up, you've got to answer it honestly.

Let's dive a little deeper into questions about price. Again, it is best to focus the conversation on how you can help the company overcome a problem or improve business. But questions about price may very well come up, and, as I've said, you'll have to answer. If your target executive says, "How much is it?" your response will be determined by the executive's motivation for asking. It's your job now to figure out why he or she is asking this.

Executives may ask about price because they are really hot and ready to buy, or it may be their way of disqualifying you before you are even out of the gate. To determine which it is, ask for information in return for sharing your price. Ask about the executive's budget and funding. To discuss pricing at this early stage, you need to understand the executive's intentions and ability to buy. Ask, "Based on your question, I presume you have a funded initiative for a solution to this problem, correct?"

If the executive answers yes, he or she actually might be a hot customer, so give a price range. Tell the executive that the price may fall in their budget range, according to his or her company's needs. Ask if the budget supports this and then set a meeting. You might say:

> "The price range starts at [$X] for the basics and [$Y] for additional deliverables. During our meeting, we will confirm this, and I will deliver an accurate proposal. I can travel to meet with you, but first I have to prepare a cost justification for my management. Let me ask you some questions."

If the executive answers no, he or she is likely trying to disqualify you. Blurting out the price before he or she understands the value of your proposal provides something that can be held against you and lose you a chance to set up a meeting. Take the opportunity to set up a meeting by saying something like this:

> "Well, I look forward to creating a proposal with pricing. Since it's our first conversation, it's difficult to give pricing until we first know what is needed. We must meet to have an understanding of the best solution to accomplish your goals. In a thirty-minute meeting, I will be able to develop a general idea of pricing as it relates to your situation. Can we set this?"

Plant Seeds

As soon as you have secured the meeting, executive will want to get off the phone or move on to other things. You are safe for a few more seconds to ask a last question. Use this question to identify interests and goals for the meeting, which will become the seeds you will grow into a conversation when you meet. Frame your question in the spirit of preparing for the meeting. Let the executive know you will prepare for this meeting by asking an open-ended question like:

> "Just so that I can better prepare for our meeting, is there a particular concern or goal I should be aware of or an area you would like for me to focus on during the meeting? Could you tell me who else might be joining and what their interests might be as well?"

Be sure to write these answers down and look up each participant's background on LinkedIn (www.linkedin.com). This information will help you to develop a conversation-starter for when you meet.

CHAPTER 5

Recap of the Sleuth Approach

BECOMING SHERLOCK HOLMES to investigate your customers and then making first contact is the essence of the sleuth face of sales. Believe me, you'll find your sales results will improve and you'll make more money if you shy away from the traditional sales techniques that no longer work very well in today's marketplace. Remember these important concepts:

- Focus on what you can do for the customer, not on what the customer can do for you to help sell him or her something.
- To find out how you can help the customer solve a problem or improve his or her business, do ICE research to identify *industry* trends, *company* pressures, and the *executive* you ultimately want to meet.
- Make low-level ICE research calls to confirm what you've found out, or to get clues about company pressures you can use in getting access to the target executive.
- Host web conferences, industry forums, and industry events to get your name in front of customers in a nonsales setting.
- Based on your research, craft an impact statement that identifies the problem or another approach you think will get you through to the decision maker. Remember to use the I-We-You format.

- Send a short e-mail containing your impact statement to the target executive, and say you'll be calling to follow up on the e-mail.
- Call the target executive and engage him or her by voicing your idea about how you can help the company. Set the meeting.

Now that you've set the meeting, it's time to take the next step and meet the doctor face of sales.

Part 2

The Doctor Face

When you meet the customer, be a doctor.

CHAPTER 6

Doctor Examination

CUSTOMERS ARE WATCHING you closely during your initial meetings and can smell insincerity a mile away. They can also sense when you're sincerely trying to improve their business or solve a vexing problem as a partner—a coconspirator, if you will. The customer knows if you're trying to sweet-talk your way to a lucrative sale or if you're a straight shooter genuinely trying to help. You want to come across as the salesperson the customer values, not the one who appears to be out solely to make the sale and cash the commission check.

Julie did this by holding a series of meetings that coauthored the customer's vision to ideally improve market share and grab a bigger piece of the pie, and so can you. Focusing your questions to benefit the customer when you meet will enhance your chances of increasing your personal value currency.

Just how do you go about increasing your personal value currency in an initial meeting? The answer is simple: stay focused on how you can help the customer solve a problem and/or improve his or her situation. The doctor analogy is quite fitting in this regard. Doctors help people who are sick. It's your job to know how you assist the customer in addressing whatever issues are on the table. Thus, the first stage of the meeting is already set. You just have to stay with a doctor-like approach so that he or she feels it was a meaningful meeting. The doctor knows how to gain customers' trust so he or she will open up and share privileged information. When you have something of value to bring to the customer, they will actually tell you a lot and give you an invitation to return!

Let's take another look at Julie's work for my software company to get a better idea of what I'm talking about.

Learning from Julie

I was in my office going over sales reports when Julie knocked on my door. She asked if she could come in to discuss a problem. I waved her in and told her to take a seat. We exchanged a few pleasantries, and then we got down to business. "What's on your mind?" I asked.

"It happened again," Julie reported. "Things were moving along just fine in the meeting with this company until their project manager interrupted with the 'why don't you just show me your product' question."

Julie's new customers would often cut the meeting short, dodge her questions, or ask to jump ahead to our product. Why was this? I knew Julie was always well-prepared when she set off to meet a customer for the first time. She was usually confident that she'd done all that she could to ask questions and uncover the customers' needs. It was a mystery, then, why the customer seemed to put up walls or back away completely.

As I reflected on Julie's performance in these initial meetings, I came to realize that the "when" factor was again the culprit. Even though Julie knew what action to take—asking questions—her lack of success occurred because she made a misstep on the "when" of asking them.

"When": Asking Too Soon without Sleuthing

Sometimes, Julie's questions to the customer stymied the meeting's progress. With the idea that customers want to talk about themselves, Julie moved too fast when skipping her sleuthing and getting to this meeting. She took an old-school, lazy approach and neglected to form a sleuth hypothesis before she walked in.

As a result, she asked questions that forced the customer to do the work on her behalf, such as, "Please tell me what keeps you up at night" or "Please tell me about your needs." Today's customers don't have time for this, and they're not fooled by the sales gambit of asking an open-ended perfunctory question. Asking these kinds of fluffy cookie-cutter questions irritates the savvy customer, who incorrectly assumes Julie has done little preparation and is trying to fake her way through the meeting.

"When": Qualifying Too Soon without Earning

In other cases, Julie would ask her qualifying questions too early in her initial meeting. Like any good salesperson, Julie didn't want to waste her efforts, so she would try to determine if the opportunity before her was real. Asking her qualifying questions too soon in the initial meeting, however, did damage. While it's human nature to focus on what's in it for you and not go into the meeting with the needs of your customer foremost in your mind, that can be a fatal mistake.

Julie would lead with questions like these:

- "So what's your budget?"
- "Are you the decision maker?"

- "How big is this going to be?"
- "When would you like to buy?"
- "Who is my competition?"

Customers had to endure this barrage of self-serving questions that benefited her sales commission but did not help them solve their problems. The customers knew that these same old canned questions didn't benefit them but were only asked to sell them something. They did not appreciate having their time wasted by her self-centered interrogation. Customers left the meeting frustrated—not the impression Julie had hoped to leave them with.

A Doctor Mind-Set

Everything changed when I told Julie, "Focus on how the customer does things now and learn their vision to improve it."

During an initial meeting, the customer is interviewing the salesperson and watching closely. He or she is trying to determine if there is value in having the salesperson come back for another meeting. The customer is cautiously optimistic, thinking, *I'm hopeful but skeptical that this sales rep will really understand and care about my business situation and not waste my time. Does she really want to help me or does she just want to make a sale?*

You are walking a fine line in this initial meeting. First, the customer needs to find value in this meeting before he or she will commit to meeting again. At the same time, you need to learn as much as you can about the customer's situation in order to determine if there is a potential sale. So this meeting is a delicate balance of both of you sizing each other up.

To handle any first meeting, Julie needed an altruistic mind-set that put customers at the center of attention. When she solely focused on understanding how customers arrived in their situation, everything changed in her favor. The customers viewed the meeting as a refreshing and valuable use of their time, while Julie gained privileged insight about the sales opportunity—information that the competition didn't have, and information that she could use to differentiate our proposal later. This intense focus on customer activities requires a mind-set like that of a doctor.

CHAPTER 7

Navigating the Initial Meeting

THE SALESPERSON WITH the doctor face looks at the customer as a patient who is seeking help. When you think about the initial meeting like a doctor's appointment, you create a conversation with the customer (patient) by asking questions that help you understand his or her situation and problems in order to recommend a solution (prescription). Like a doctor, you will diagnose the customer's situation in an interactive conversation that entails asking questions that benefit the customer, not you.

Your Personal Value Currency

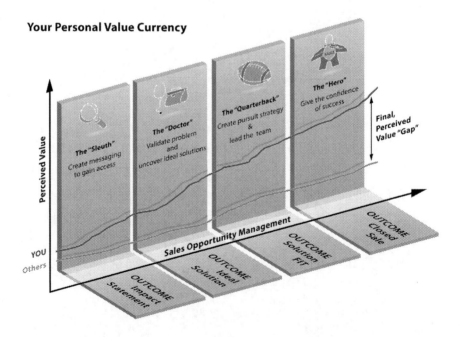

Your personal value currency can skyrocket when you handle this meeting like a doctor. To really differentiate yourself, you must create a conversation like a doctor to a patient. Do this by asking questions that get the customer to envision and articulate ways of improving his or her situation (more on this later), qualify the problem as one worth solving, and motivate the customer to take action.

This meeting is not about talking. If you feel you will only have this one meeting to tell your story and you have a head full of data to deliver, the temptation is to talk nonstop to be sure you get it all in. You're focusing on discussing a solution before the customer is ready to hear it. Salespeople with this charge-ahead attitude open their meeting with an information dump. They love to talk and tell stories from their own perspective—*tell, tell, tell.* They never shut up.

Avoiding an "information dump" on your initial meeting is essential to building your personal value currency.

Over and over again, I have seen this approach aggravate customers and cause them to be hesitant to ask questions for fear of having to sit through a long-winded lecture for an answer. In their mind, all they want to do is get you to *stop talking* so they can end the meeting. Do not get anxious or impatient. When your customer says, "We feel we need to do XYZ," *do not* jump right in to announce you have product ABC that can do just that. *Do not* take the attitude of, "I have just the thing for you!" This impatience kills your personal value currency.

There are four essential steps you'll need to take to successfully navigate initial meetings with target executives:

1. **Make Them Smile:** Set the tone of the meeting by making it clear it will be about the customer, not about you.
2. **Establish Control:** Take control of the meeting by establishing the purpose, to which the customer agrees.
3. **Get Them Talking:** Give some information about what you know of the customer's situation and get him or her to elaborate.
4. **Create a Vision:** Create a safe environment for the customer to collaborate, and coauthor an ideal solution with which to solve his or her problem.

Let's look at each of these steps in more detail.

Make Them Smile

In the initial moments of your meeting, the customer is carefully observing how you come across and will make quick judgments about you. Customers have their antennae up, wondering, *Are you looking out for me to solve my problem or are you trying to make a sale?* To focus the customer and get a feel for his or her personality, say something like this:

"Thank you so much for taking the time to meet with me today." Now be quiet.

It's easy to make a poor first impression if you try too hard to build rapport. A typical mistake happens if you are too eager to break the silence and blurt out comments about the personal items you see in the customer's office—like remarking on the customer's family photos or a bowling trophy on the desk. In the early minutes of your initial meeting, it is risky to assume the customer is ready or interested in discussing any personal topics with you. If you make a comment on this too early, it can backfire, since you may be perceived as using a disingenuous sales ploy. Instead, keep any personal comments to yourself and focus on the business at hand. Another mistake is to say a seemingly harmless thing like, "I believe there's a way I can be of service to the company, and I'm looking forward to talking with you about it." Wow. In your first seconds of the meeting you already irked the customer by coming across with the presumption that you expect to sell him or her something. That's quite a turnoff.

Keep your initial doctor meetings about business and nothing personal.

Look out for the customer's response to determine his or her personality type. The way customers answer this opening rapport comment will allow you to peg their personality type. To build positive rapport, act like a mirror and simply reflect the customer's personality type back to him or her. Here are the four personality types to observe and reflect back like a mirror:

1. **Straight Shooter:** This type moves fast and wants to get right down to business. These customers will give concise and direct answers to your opening rapport comments. *To reflect their personality back:* Take out your notepad and pen right away and begin the meeting.

2. **Chatty Cathy:** This type smiles and acts friendly, with a goal of keeping your meeting positive. These customers will likely ramble an answer to your opening rapport comment. *To reflect their personality back:* Let them talk. Smile, listen

patiently, and wait until they are finished to get down to business.

3. **Loud and Proud:** This type is ambitious and driven to receive recognition and attention from their company. These customers will take your opening rapport comment as an opportunity to share business accomplishments and sometimes hint that others don't know what they're doing. *To reflect their personality back:* Highlight your mutual business goal for their achievement and leading-edge response to situations.

4. **The Librarian:** This type is focused on facts and figures and does not like taking risks. These customers may ignore your opening rapport comment or give a vague answer. *To reflect their personality back:* Share how you will be cautious in presenting any ideas, using only the facts to make improvements.

Naturally, personality types that are most like your own are the easiest to reflect back. For instance, if you are a straight shooter and your customer is a straight shooter, it's quite easy to reflect that personality type by getting down to business quickly and keeping the rapport discussion to a minimum. However, difficulties arise when it comes to opposite personality types. If you are a straight shooter and your customer is a chatty Cathy who likes to spend time getting to know you, it might be difficult reflecting his or her personality. These customers tend to be more loquacious, while you want to get to the point. Your opposite type requires a more deliberate and conscious effort in order to make a connection.

Establish Control

Take control in an elegant way by stating the purpose of the meeting for the customer's agreement. The purpose of your doctor meeting is to assess the customer's situation and explore ways to help. Therefore, this will be a conversation about the customer—not a presentation of your products. Agree on the purpose upfront and prepare the customer to answer your questions in a collaborative conversation.

Once you arrive in the meeting room, customers may sit down with their arms folded expecting you to show them something. Consider any discussion on the purpose of the meeting as a mini-negotiation to establish this first upfront agreement. The purpose statement will guide the customer's expectations of the meeting and set the tone to avoid any surprises or misunderstandings. For example, you might say:

> "I would like to confirm that the purpose of today's meeting is to discuss your current situation and goals in order to come back with a solution. Therefore, I will be asking questions to better understand your situation and discuss ideas. Based on what we learn together, we can mutually determine if and how to best proceed. Does this sound good, or do you have any additions or changes you would like to make?"

Get Them Talking

After making introductions and agreeing on the purpose of the meeting, get the customer talking. With a mind-set of understanding the customer rather than being understood, you are asking questions and listening for 80 percent of this conversation.

Give to Get

You need to give customers something in order to increase their willingness to answer your questions. You only have one thing to offer: your hypothesis from sleuth research. If you delivered an impact statement during a previous sleuth conversation you can also use the seeds that you planted about the customer's interests. In either case, you will need to give this as your conversation starter. This knowledge is now an asset to prime the conversation and warm up the customer for answering questions. Say something like this:

> "Based on our research and previous conversations with others in your company, we understand that a recent audit prompted your CEO to mandate an initiative toward improving operational effectiveness."

You have to earn the right to get answers to your questions from the customer. If you start the conversation by blurting out your questions, the customer may feel defensive and avoid your questions with vague or short answers.

"Can You Elaborate?"

With a positive and curious tone, ask the customer to share more about his or her situation. Use the approach "Tell me more about …" to ask the customer to describe and elaborate upon the situation. This is an open-ended question that encourages the customer to explain rather than answer yes or no. Here are some examples:

- "Please tell me more about what you mean about improving this."
- "Please elaborate about how you define an improvement."
- "Please describe how you are experiencing challenges."

"How Do You Do Things?"

Be careful not to just sit there and ask, "What are your needs?" When you ask this question, you are making customers do all the work to figure out what they need. Think about it—does your doctor ever walk in and ask you what you "need"? Never. That's because doctors know that we rely on them to determine what we need after we describe our situation. The same is true with the customer as you have this doctor meeting. Customers know a lot about their situation but little about what they need to do to solve it. It's really up to you to figure out what they need, based on the way they do things. To uncover that information, ask how, when, where, and why questions:

- "How is the process being done now?"
- "When do you encounter issues?"
- "Where do the breakdowns occur?"
- "Why do you do things this way?"

As the customer speaks, listen intently by concentrating on what is being said and visibly take notes to make the customer feel like he or she has been heard. Nod to encourage customers to talk about how they do things while you take notes. Pay attention instead of planning your next statement. Pounce on answers and ask for clarification: "I'm not sure I'm clear on what you meant by that. Can you elaborate?"

Chalk Talk

When the customer is done giving answers, it's showtime. This show will be your chalk talk, which simply means that you are going to write on a whiteboard. (If there is no whiteboard, simply move next to the customer and take out a blank sheet of paper.)

Ask for permission to use the whiteboard. Stand up and bring your notes to the whiteboard and write "How We Do Things" on top. While referring to your notes, rephrase what you heard the customer tell you and write those items on the board in bullet-point form. If applicable, draw illustrations that reflect how the customer described the company's current process. While you do this, say:

> "So what I heard you saying is that these are the three points that are contributing to your situation … correct?"

It's important to note that this move will build personal value currency with your contact person, which is very important. The exercise of writing down what was said on the whiteboard is meant to make the customer feel that he or she has been heard and understood.

Keep rephrasing for clarification until they say, "Yes, that's it. That's what I mean."

Encourage the customer to speak while you listen like a doctor.

- Pounce on each sentence the customer says and rephrase it until you get it right. "So, what I hear you saying is …"
- You might say, "I'm not sure I am clear on what you meant by [X]. Can you give me an example?"
- Continue to rephrase and don't be afraid to be wrong. You might say this four times and get it wrong until the fifth time the customer says, "Yes, that's what I mean."

Create a Vision

Now that you know about how the customer does things, prompt him or her to imagine how those things can be done better. What is a better way to get things done? When the customer thinks about success in improving the company's situation, what does it look like in his or her mind? Is there an ideal state of how things could be better? The answer to these questions defines the customer's ideal solution.

> **Coauthor the customer's ideal solution,**
> **and you'll build personal value currency**
> **that you will need to spend later.**

Walk back to the whiteboard. In front of everyone, write "Ideal Solution" next to "How We Do Things." While writing this, ask the customer to describe an ideal state of how the company could "do things better." Ask plainly:

"What is your vision of an ideal way to improve this situation? What would an ideal solution look like to be a success? If you had a paintbrush, how would you paint your ideal solution?"

Since the customer's ideal solution is based on his or her opinions, thoughts, and views, ask follow-up questions.

- "In your opinion, what are your thoughts regarding _____?"
- "What's your view about _____?"
- "Where are you versus where you want to be?"
- "How will you know you have been successful?"
- "What factors are contributing to the current situation?"
- "What will things look like with your ideal solution in place?"
- "What has worked or not worked so far to address this?"

Invite the customer to join you at the whiteboard. Being elbow-to-elbow looking at the board is a crucial part of collaboration. It influences the customer's vision of you as a coauthor of the ideal solution. By letting the customer collaborate, you empower him or her to speak freely. Your actions and questions will encourage the customer to "think out loud" about an ideal solution, which will help him or her articulate opinions, thoughts, and views. Your questions and illustrations help the customer become more aware and enlightened. In this way, you're truly acting as the doctor.

Bite your lip if the customer claims to want something your product can do. Stay cool. If your customer says, "We feel we need to improve these areas," don't jump in to exclaim, "That's great, because we have just the product that can do that!" Similarly, if the customer says something that your product can't do, don't panic. Avoid the temptation to dive in and prove him or her wrong. If the customer says, "We don't think we need to fix that area of the process," don't jump in and say, "Well, you should!" This puts up defenses and inhibits your ability to have an open conversation. Whatever the customer says, simply smile, nod, and quietly write it under "Ideal Solution."

Congratulations! You've now almost won over your customer. You have certainly created personal value currency that you'll need in the next phase of the initial meeting, which we'll discuss in the next chapter.

CHAPTER 8

Making a Prognosis

THE DOCTOR MEETING is a two-way street. Your customer must benefit from your questions, and you must benefit from knowing if the opportunity is real. It's really that simple.

So far, all of your questions have been designed to help the customer collaborate and create a vision of an ideal solution. Now you have earned the right to ask questions that will help you qualify the opportunity. You are about to spend more of your company's time and resources, should you decide to set additional meetings with the customer. Therefore, since you have a finite amount of time and resources yourself, you want to spend this on real opportunities that you can win with a profit. It's time for you to make a decision. Ask the following three questions:

1. "Is It Real?"
2. "Can I Win It?"
3. "Is It Worth the Effort?"

I will go into more detail on each question in the sections below, but suffice it to say that if the answer is yes to all three of these questions, this is a qualified opportunity and you can move forward. If any of the answers is no, this may become an unqualified opportunity, and you should consider ending your work with this customer to spend your time on only qualified opportunities. You can only really qualify an opportunity by asking these three questions which can occur in one meeting as a doctor.

It is not recommended to blurt out these qualifying questions at the beginning of your initial meeting, since asking questions that benefit you and not the customer will deplete your personal value currency. Remember, everything is about building personal value currency to get return access. A common mistake salespeople make is asking questions way too early, before they have earned any currency. Just conduct your doctor examination before you rush to qualify the opportunity—it could even be as short as thirty minutes on the phone. This way, you'll get your qualifying questions answered and still grow that vital currency.

Is It Real?

There are a number of factors you need to weigh to determine if you are pursuing a real opportunity or just someone seeking free information from you without an intent of buying anything. The benefits of the solution, the key people involved, and the costs of instituting the solution versus doing nothing are all considerations. Below is a series of questions that go into the equation. In addition, I'll discuss the different types of people within the company who will be involved in the decision-making process.

What Are the Benefits of Solving the Problem?

The key question you want answered definitively at the first meeting is, how will the customer benefit from solving the problem? You need to determine if the customer really needs to solve this problem or if he or she can get along without solving it. A benefit gauge will determine the benefits of solving the customer's problem. The gauge is only about the customer solving the problem, not about your solution. Ask these questions:

- "Can you help me to understand how a solution will benefit your company?"
- "What will happen if this issue or problem isn't resolved?"

As your customer speaks, take out your calculator and create a benefit gauge in front of him or her. With any solution (not just yours) in place, the customer may reduce costs, increase revenue, increase productivity, and improve competitiveness. This gauge will also be needed in the next face of sales for your presentation.

Qualify the Problem: "The Benefit Gauge"

Who Is Involved in Solving the Problem?

In the course of your meetings, you will be introduced to various people who are involved in making buying decisions. Find out about all the decision stakeholders by asking about the process, not the people. Ask about the process of making decisions:

- "Besides yourself, who else in your organization will be engaged in making a decision?"
- "Can you share the process of making decisions?"
- "Who is recommending the decision, and how is it authorized and finalized?"

The answers to these questions will reveal three stakeholder roles: decision maker, influencer, and champion. It is important to determine these roles to figure out your next step, when you write the prescription.

Decision Maker

The decision maker authorizes approval and can sign the agreement. This person decides if the company will or will not commit to your proposal. This is an executive, director, head, or administrator who controls resources and expenditures. When you ask stakeholders about the process of making a decision, they will reveal the decision maker. Of course, they may be wrong, so you need to verify this by asking the same question of other stakeholders, which will corroborate this information.

Many times, when asked, stakeholders will get mixed up and think the definition of a decision maker is the person who recommends the decision. They might, therefore, think they are the decision maker when they are actually not the one who makes the commitment, but instead one who makes a recommendation—an influencer.

Beware when stakeholders mistakenly tell you they are the decision makers and you should only be talking to them. They will unintentionally mislead you because they may be under the impression that they can make a decision. These stakeholders think they're powerful and you should recognize them. You can honor that, but don't make the mistake of believing a person to be the decision maker unless he or she has the actual authority to finalize the agreement. Verify his or her claim by making sure that higher-level management isn't involved in the decision.

Reveal whether or not this person is the true decision maker by asking, "Are there any other higher-level management involved in authorizing the decision, or is that you?"

Influencer

These are the stakeholders who are not actually making the decision but are asked by the decision maker for input. They are called decision influencers. Influencers surround the decision maker to provide advice regarding your solution.

Some influencers have more power than others. They might have expertise on a topic, which makes them powerful and important for the decision maker to listen to their recommendation—such as the technical expert who knows more about the technology than anyone else. No one can argue against these influencers, since no one knows what they know. This can also be the person who is well respected (or well liked) as someone who does a lot for the company—such as carry a heavy workload, generate revenue, or solve tough customer problems.

These are power influencers. The decision maker will likely listen to the power influencers and take their advice. The power influencers can't make the decision but are more influential in the decision-making process with the decision maker. Power influencers can influence the decision maker either directly or indirectly even without a big title. The decision maker will ask for their opinion and will trust their judgment.

To identify your power influencer, ask another influencer about the various relationships between the decision maker and influencers. Ask, "Can you let me know how the decision maker weighs the information from the various people involved? Does the decision maker seek a consensus of influencers or seek advice from certain individuals with expertise?" The answers will give you insight into the executive's trust level with the various influencers and will highlight the ones you most need to focus on.

Champion

Among your decision stakeholders, there is usually one person who emerges to become your ally, someone who is on your side and is in favor of your solution. This is your champion. Keep your eye out to identify your champion.

What is your champion's clout to influence other decision stakeholders? This depends on the ability of your champion to mobilize others in the company to form a consensus. How much clout does he or she have within the company to get things done? Would that individual have the leadership to motivate others in the company to take action in your favor? Ask, "How confident or concerned are you that the other stakeholders will follow your lead in a decision?"

You can provide the champion with statistics, case studies, and relevant data that he or she can distribute to the other influencers. Your constant feeding of this information will help the champion explain why your solution is a good fit. Treat your champion well, since he or she will become a vital partner for you in the next phases (quarterback and hero).

Create a stakeholder map—which is an organizational chart of all the people involved in the decision—to keep track of all the stakeholders in the decision process as well as his or her respective ideal solution that you uncovered during your doctor examination.

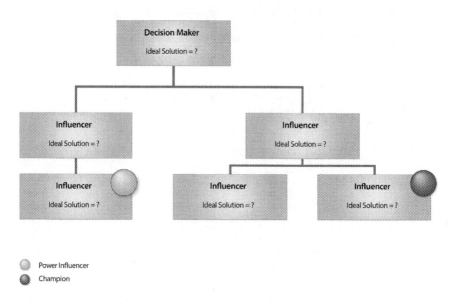

How Important Is It to Solve the Problem?

It might be a problem to some stakeholders, but other stakeholders may believe it's not important enough to make the effort to solve it.

Therefore, it may be difficult to get the support and funding for the customer to implement a solution. Ask these questions:

- "Where on your priority list is this problem to solve?"
- "Is the solution on your top list this year or this quarter?"
- "What about your management's priorities?"
- "What is the process of obtaining funds for this initiative?"
- "Are there any risks of this initiative going unfunded?"

Can I Win It?

Here you have to size up your chances of winning the sale. Naturally, your offering will have strengths and weaknesses in comparison to other alternatives. Here you need to find how what is most important to them in their ideal solution. Ask how important the following aspects of their ideal solution are:

1. An innovative solution?
   o How important is it for them to have vendor innovations ahead of the marketplace?

2. A solution with support?
   o How important is the support and people to solve any issues and deploy resources?

3. A solution that has been proven?
   o How important is it for them to succeed within their own company by keeping the solution-users happy?

Now, if your company is strong at any other than these three solutions above and it's also important to the customer, then that's good news—you have a good chance to be a good fit. To the contrary, if your company strengths are, in fact, not important to the customer, then this might not be a qualified opportunity.

Is It Worth the Effort?

If you win the business, it will be a good sale only if the customer agrees to a price that is profitable for your company and for its success. Will your customer pay for value, or is he or she only looking for a cheap price? Will the customer invest in services and staff to support the delivery of a solution or does he or she want to go it alone? Ask these questions:

- "How important is price in your decision?"
- "Will your company pay more for an innovative, proven solution with support (from above) or are you looking for the lowest price?"

Now if your company does not offer the lowest price in the market, and the customer says this is the most important factor in a buying decision, you will have to decide: stop pursuit since this is unqualified or pursue this opportunity and challenge this notion during the next quarterback face (more on this later).

CHAPTER 9

The Doctor's Prescription

WITH MEDICAL TREATMENTS, there typically are a number of options. That's true in advancing the sales opportunity as well. Think about it: The doctor knows that the patient has no idea what to do next, so it is the doctor's job to make a prescription and give instructions on how things will go. You never hear a doctor ask, "So, what would you like to do next?" Doctors don't ask what to do—they tell the patient what to do. That is exactly what you must tactfully do now.

As you take control, you're not pushing the customer to take action. Instead, imagine yourself putting an arm around the customer and pointing to the cure. You are pulling the customer along, with full disclosure, on the road ahead.

> **You are controlling the process but not the customer. Take control of the process by pulling him or her to the next face.**

Option 1: Advance to Quarterback

We'll discuss the quarterback face of sales in greater detail in the next chapter. For our purposes here, let's just say that the next face involves presenting the solution and responding to what you've learned thus far. Your first prescription would entail making such a decision. Do you want to advance to the next phase?

Advance to the quarterback face of sales if you have a qualified opportunity plus the ideal solution from every decision stakeholder. Say, "Based on this meeting, we can present our solution as it aligns with everyone's opinions, thoughts, and views."

Deciding to advance, or not, will get easier as you gain more experience as a doctor.

You have not presented anything yet. You are growing trust (personal value currency) by collaborating and coauthoring solutions as the doctor, with the customer's vision in mind. This gives you a key asset—the customer's ideal solution, which is the ammunition for your presentation as the quarterback. Otherwise, you go in presenting with no idea what the customer has in mind and take a wild guess as to what is needed. You risk looking foolish if you present without knowing the customer's ideal solution.

You may need only one thirty-minute doctor meeting to accomplish this. The whole purpose of this doctor face is to have a conversation and collaborate on the customer's ideal solution. It's to coauthor the ideal vision for solving the customer's problem. Get the customer to think out loud and use his or her imagination on how life could be better if the problem was solved. As the doctor, you are getting the patient to participate in recognizing the best ways to solve his or her problem.

Option 2: Stay as the Doctor

If you have a qualified opportunity but do not know the ideal solution from every decision stakeholder, keep this opportunity in the doctor face until you do. Each stakeholder has personal opinions, thoughts, and views about the ideal solution. You need to take the time to learn about each stakeholder's ideal solution. If you don't know the spoken words regarding every stakeholder's ideal solution, then don't advance. Resist the temptation to present your product without the full picture. Resist the urge to jump the gun. You may regret going full steam ahead without laying the groundwork first.

A problem can arise if you make assumptions about certain stakeholders and their ideal solution when you have not talked with them. Making these assumptions about certain stakeholders can leave you blind when you present your solution. Don't take shortcuts; talk to all the stakeholders and hear their own ideal solutions. No matter how confident you feel, you must make sure to learn this from all stakeholders associated with the decision-making process.

Steer the conversation around to asking the customer to set a meeting with other stakeholders before a presentation. Say something like this:

> "Based on this meeting, I recommend we set another meeting with a few others to determine their respective opinions, thoughts, and views and how they align with what we've learned here."

To make this request, position yourself to benefit other stakeholders the same way you benefited the customer during his or her doctor meetings. This way, he or she views introducing you to others as a way to use your and your skills (like a doctor) to work on the stakeholders' behalf. You will be a facilitator to meeting the other stakeholders and reconciling their ideal solutions. You are of value to this customer because of the way you are handling this meeting. You have benefited your customer by getting him or her to think and articulate his or her ideal solution. Your skills as the doctor got him or her to open up. Therefore, your customer will be comfortable bringing you to others in order to map out ideal solutions as well. It's all about you—you are the important factor. Not your product, but how you handled this meeting. You have earned the right to ask for this.

Don't be afraid to defer the presentation of your solution until you have the ideal solution from all stakeholders.

There will be times when you will be uncomfortable doing this since it's against your instincts to present your solution—I know you are raring to go and show your product whenever you have a chance. It's even more difficult if your customer is asking you for a presentation. You naturally want to do what the customer tells you instead of recommending that you first meet the other stakeholders. Recommending this to the customer, at first glance, may seem like pushing your luck. This may be true if you used the traditional approach of begging for a meeting and asking questions that benefit you to qualify and sell the customer at his or her expense. But you didn't. You didn't beg him or her for a meeting like the usual salesperson; you shared a new idea or hypothesis. You didn't just ask questions to help sell them; you asked questions to help him or her articulate his or her thoughts, feelings, and opinions. As a result, after this initial doctor meeting, your personal value currency should have a major jolt upward. They are feeling close to you. You have to count on this in order to ask for this next step.

Quid Pro Quo

Either prescription will cost you and your company time and effort. Therefore, you need to ask for something in return. This is your quid pro quo, meaning a comparable exchange or barter of your effort for something you want in return. It's a favor for a favor. What will the customer give you in return for allocating your resources on his or her behalf? You might ask the customer to assemble other stakeholders, socialize your different ideal solution ideas to other stakeholders, or arrange a customer reference call and distribute a case study. Here's something you could say:

> "We are happy to invest our resources to prepare for our next meeting, where we'll present the solution more in full. In return, we would like to confirm we can meet with your colleagues involved with this decision. Okay?"

CHAPTER 10

Recap of the Doctor Approach

LET'S REVIEW WHAT we learned in the doctor face of sales before we move on to the next phase of the sales process.

- Listen and get the customer talking, but don't present your solution in full. You're mining for new information that will help you make the sale.
- Avoid an information dump about your service or product.
- Ask how the customer does things, not what the customer needs.
- Encourage the customer to share opinions, thoughts, and views about his or her ideal solution.
- Collaborate with the customer to come up with an ideal solution to the problem. Write notes on a whiteboard and confirm your understanding of everything the customer said.
- Qualify the customer as a potential opportunity.
- Don't move on to your full presentation until you have spoken to all stakeholders about what they think regarding the issue or problem you are all trying to address.

Success in your initial customer meetings is all about careful listening with the sincere goal of helping your customer. If you do both very well, you'll build your personal value currency early on and boost the chances of closing the deal.

Part 3

The Quarterback Face

When you present your product, be a quarterback.

CHAPTER 11

Quarterback Challenge

CUSTOMERS BECOME ANNOYED when they have to sit though sales presentations that have nothing to do with their own vision and views. The quarterback knows how to present and bring new ideas that take the customer's views into consideration. Julie secured agreement with decision stakeholders that our product was the best way to accomplish their goal and solve their problem. You can do the same with your service or product.

Learning from Julie

"Thanks for the nice presentation. We'll get back to you."

Julie had finished another presentation and, with the customer's response, was back in "maybe" land once again. Maybe they'd liked what she had to say; maybe they hadn't. The customer was politely unclear and never offered any of the straight answers Julie hoped for. What happened? Where did she stand?

Julie's presentations seemed to go well and according to plan. She always walked into her meetings with a clear understanding of what the customer was looking for in the presentation. She was confident and upbeat. However, afterward, she would receive blank stares without much dialogue or questioning. Things always seemed to come to a sharp halt when Julie finished speaking. If she knew what the customer wanted and presented it well, how could things turn out this way so often?

As I looked back and reflected on Julie's presentations, I began to see that once again, the "when" elements were Julie's downfall. While Julie knew what action to take—presenting her proposed solution based on the customer's needs—I discovered that she erred in deciding when to engage the customer during the presentation.

"When": Talking Too Long about Your Solution

At times, Julie would talk too much about her presentation and forgot to put the customer's situation front and center. She would roll into her meeting and begin the presentation with a talk about the greatness of her company and her proposed solution, all accompanied by bright, colorful slides. Instead of making a case for new ideas based on the customer's vision, Julie in essence delivered a long-winded advertisement, complete with lots of facts and figures, without ever making any connection to previous discussions. While customers started the meeting feeling optimistic and attentive, their interest waned when they didn't hear anything related to their situation.

Julie missed the opportunity to engage her audience when she rambled on with a generic, self-absorbed presentation. Without realizing it, Julie lost her connection with the customer by delaying the most critical piece of the presentation, the part that was all about the customer's vision and needs and how her solution could meet them. In these cases, Julie lost some of her personal value currency.

"When": Too Fast to Assume Agreement

At other times, Julie was too quick to assume the customer agreed with her presentation. Using her assumptive approach, Julie intentionally acted as if the customer had already deemed her presentation a success. She'd close her talk with something along the lines of, "As you can see, the logical choice is for you to embrace this opportunity with us. I'm sure you will agree that our solution clearly meets your needs. So, let's get the paperwork started for a proposal. Do you prefer standard product or premium?" When customers would answer this question, Julie incorrectly interpreted it as a sign that they approved of her approach.

In reality, Julie's approach backfired. By assuming the customer approved without allowing a discussion, Julie intended to make it difficult for the customer to bring up any negative questions. She believed her enthusiasm would be contagious and squash the customer's objections, but by behaving in this way, what she really squashed was any opportunity for open, honest dialogue. Julie did real damage to her relationship with her now aggravated customers, leaving them to believe she was presumptuous, disrespectful, and attempting to bulldoze them into agreeing with her.

A Quarterback Mind-Set

When I told Julie, "Remember everything the customer told you and now challenge them to look for new ways to solve their problem," everything changed.

The quarterback sales face is all about making a connection with customers and challenging their views previously expressed during the doctor face.

You are in the spotlight. Your presentation is your moment to shine and build on your personal value currency. Having spent time discussing the customer's situation during your doctor meetings, you are now expected to deliver a relevant presentation in response to what you've learned. Customers are now optimistic that you will impress them and are likely to be thinking: *I hope you listened to what I told you and won't let me down. I am expecting this presentation will provide a clear vision of new ideas and ways for me to address my situation in the best way.*

You are ready for this moment because you have a unique understanding of the customer's ideal solution. The customer delivered this privileged insight on a silver platter during your doctor meetings. It's time to capitalize on your intelligence asset by putting it front and center in your presentation. When you highlight customers' spoken words upfront, you immediately engage them, and they will listen to your presentation.

You'll need to create a relevant and clear response that takes the customer's ideal solution into consideration. This presentation must challenge customers to consider your proposed solution to be the best way to solve their problem, although it may differ from the ideal solution they had in mind. You will need a new mind-set while preparing to deliver these challenges to influence the customer to agree with your point of view.

In football, the quarterback is the highly visible leader of the team. With poise under pressure, the quarterback must challenge the opponent throughout the game so that his team can score. As you don the face of the quarterback, you, too, will engage and challenge the customer—your "opponent" during this phase—so that he or she will come to see that your solution is a good fit for the problem at hand. Score!

As I mentioned, it is important for you to move from the doctor face of the sales process into the quarterback face. In the quarterback face, you craft your presentation in a way that will engage customers with new ideas to solve their problems. As a result, the customer will feel validated that you listened and be more open to your solutions. The customer's positive feelings will, in turn, continue to build your personal value currency. Let's take the field and get you ready to make your presentation like a quarterback.

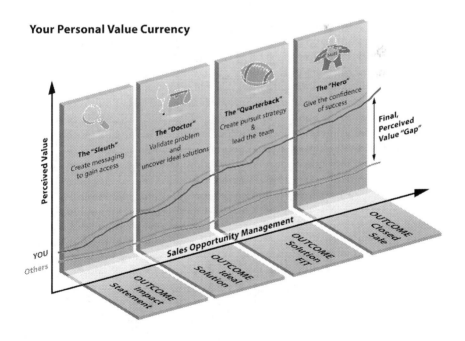

CHAPTER 12

Play the Game

BEGIN THE QUARTERBACK part of your presentation with a recap of your customer's situation. This is what customers want to hear first and foremost—that the whole exercise is all about them! They are wondering if you really listened to what they told you during your doctor meetings. Using a few slides, share your understanding of the customer's situation and the benefit gauge you created during your doctor meetings. Say something like:

> "Based on our meetings, we understand you have initiated an effort to improve your business. By making improvements in your department, your goal is to improve productivity by 20 percent. We have validated this goal as a key defense against your emerging competitors in new markets. A recent *Harvard Business Review* article points out that there are a dozen new competitors taking away from your market share each year. You can expect to fend off these emerging competitors in new markets."

Present Your Customer's Ideal Solution

Using notes from your doctor meetings, you'll put the customer's spoken words in quotes on your slides and read them out loud to describe his or her ideal solution for solving his or her problem. For example:

> "We listened carefully when you told us that your ideal solution is an innovative product with an expert level of support and a price that is within your budget. We have been thinking about your ideal solution at length with our team, and have prepared our proposed solution accordingly."

The Game Plan

With the ideal solution in full sight of the customer, you'll take out your game plan. Your game plan will outline the four elements that will solve the customer's problem as it relates to his or her ideal solution:

1. your innovative company
2. your exceptional people
3. your proven product
4. your balanced price

Present each of these four elements, one by one, to demonstrate how your solution is a good fit with the customer's ideal solution. After you present each element, solicit customers' feedback by asking if they see it as a good fit. Ask these questions:

- "When you said your ideal solution included this aspect, is this what you meant?"
- "Have I demonstrated our capabilities in alignment with your vision?"

The answers to your questions, repeated over the course of all four elements, will reveal if your solution is a good fit or not. Your goal is to have the customer say "yes" to these questions throughout your presentation, establishing four small agreements toward an overall good fit.

"Our (Innovative) Company"

The customer should select you because of your company's ability to deliver innovations ahead of the marketplace. In doing so, customers won't become locked in with a company that cannot keep pace with their future needs.

If you are selling products or services in which innovation can help the customer, your case will be easier to make. This is important to the customer because lack of innovation has ramifications. In most cases, you can think creatively to make innovation important. If you sell technology-related products or services, this is easier since a lag time for innovation can cost him or her. But any product or service can have a story around how innovation is important. If you have a commodity product or service, perhaps focus on the technology and the innovation of actually creating it. Even though the product is always the same, the process of making it is where you highlight innovation.

**When playing the role of quarterback,
you're selling yourself as much as you're selling the
customer on your company.**

Highlight how your company has been producing innovative solutions (or innovative ways to manufacture and distribute them) that will provide advantages for your customers. A few slides should highlight success stories, case studies, or testimonials that illustrate how your solution has helped other customers. Present your company's background and mission, growth rate (if it's positive), awards or recognized industry accolades, and a customer list within the industry. Point out how your company's ongoing commitment to continuous improvement will help meet customers' future needs, even those they might not even anticipate now. With alternative solutions, they will be "boxed in," waiting around for innovation while their competitors are moving ahead with your solution.

Sample Script

"My company was founded with a mission to improve results and has been recognized as a leader by several analysts. We have over two hundred customers globally and have grown more than 20 percent per year over the past three years. My company has several customers in your industry, dealing with the same situation that you are facing. One customer in your industry utilized our solution and realized improved results within the first two months of implementation. Their 30 percent improvement gains paid for our solution within the first year.

During our meetings, you told me that your ideal solution includes a company that is investing in innovation to anticipate your long-term needs. Consider our company your partner in solving today's problem while we also make ongoing improvements to help you preempt future challenges. While other companies may seek to emulate our innovations several months or years later, does your company really want to wait around for a copycat alternative? Consider the negative ramifications of waiting. With our expertise and proven track record, our company continues to strengthen and widen the gap between ourselves and the weaker copycats. They simply cannot keep pace with our advancements."

- *Ask,* "Have I demonstrated our capabilities in alignment with your vision?"

"Our (Exceptional) People"

The customer should select you because of the support and people you will bring to solve any issues—most importantly, your ability to marshal resources. This is important to customers because delivery is not as easy as they might think, and issues will always come up. They will need a team they can trust to get the job done right and overcome inevitable obstacles.

Emphasize the importance of your track record for on-time delivery. Also, emphasize how your experienced support team will respond, along with your ability to marshal resources when something goes wrong. Your ability to marshal resources from within your company is the most important value you can provide the customer. This enables you to take responsibility, deploy your support staff from within your company, and help customers respond to issues. It is critical that you highlight your ability to get things done and deploy resources on the customer's behalf when problems arise.

People are behind the success or failure of a company, so selling on your company's stellar human resources is a big plus.

Sample Script

"During our meetings, you told me that your ideal solution includes a support team that delivers what it promises to get you up and running on time. Your solution is more complex to implement than most others would know. With our experienced local support team, we can make it look easy. We have delivery and support staff on standby, ready to support you with a fast and efficient process. In addition to our support team, you can also call on me to marshal resources on your behalf if needed. My team and I will support you better than the alternatives."

- *Ask,* "Have I demonstrated our capabilities in alignment with your vision?"

"Our (Proven) Service or Product"

Customers should select you because you will make them look good within their own company by keeping the solution-users happy. Your product will give them this peace of mind by offering three capabilities: easy-to-use functionality, performance, and customization. *Easy-to-use* means that people will actually enjoy using your solution without resistance. *Performance* means that your product will be able to scale to support a large audience without a slowdown. *Customization* means that customers can tailor certain features and functions of your solution to their liking.

This is important to customers because without these three capabilities, their peers and management team will wonder why they chose to go with a mediocre alternative that was "good enough for now." Without easy-to-use functionality, performance, and customization, customers will have to spend a great deal of time dealing with issues and complaints from colleagues and finding ways to make them happy. Eventually, complaints from others will cause customers to regret their decision.

Sample Script

"During our meetings, you told me that your ideal solution includes high quality to support a particular audience. We define *quality* as easy-to-use functionality, performance, and customization. This is a major advantage of our product that prompts switchbacks to us from other rigid, lower-grade alternatives."

- *Ask,* "Have I demonstrated our capabilities in alignment with your vision?"

Notice that the quarterback always cites previous meetings and repeats the common agreements for emphasis, keeping you in control and building on your personal value currency.

"Our (Balanced) Price vs. Risk"

The customer should select you because you have the best price with the most value to assure success. Customers will be confident that they won't fail by trying to be too cheap and incurring massive risk.

Position any lower-priced alternatives as risky because they do not offer your company, people, and product. A good way to explain this is by showing a balance visual with "price (includes company, people, product)" on one side and "risk" on the other. As the price moves lower on one side, the risk of failure goes up—and vice versa. Demonstrate how your solution provides an attractive balance between a fair price and the lowest risk of failure.

Sample Script

"During our meetings, you told me that your ideal solution includes a vendor that provides a good price. Well, I believe I have just proven we offer the best price for the value we will deliver—based on our company, people, and product. The high value of these three differentiating benefits easily outweighs the risks."

- *Ask,* "Have I demonstrated our capabilities in alignment with your vision?"

Acting on what you learned to benefit the customer is the mark of a true professional in sales.

CHAPTER 13

Tactfully Challenging Your Customers

HERE'S THE GOOD news. A customer's vision of an ideal solution can be changed to favor what you have to offer. This is because ideal solutions are not based on fact but, rather, on customers' opinions, thoughts, and views about how they could do things better. A well-known approach (not invented here) that has been effectively used to elicit change is called "Feel-Felt-Found." Using this approach, you lead customers into unchartered, unknown, and unfamiliar territory, causing them to consider new ideas to solve their problem in favor of your offering. Here's how it works:

Feel
- Empathize with how they *feel*.
- Acknowledge your understanding of the customer's ideal solution.
- State your understanding in a broader perspective: "I understand why you feel that the long-term performance of a solution product is less important than a lower price."

Felt
- Show how others have *felt* the same way.

- Let them know that others like them have thought the same thing.
- Say, "Your opinions, thoughts, and views are similar to those of several other companies who, like you, believed a low price was more important than the long-term product performance."

Found
- Show what those other companies have *found* to be the truth.

Remember that you are the expert here, not the customer. While the customer is facing this situation for the first time, you have seen how other companies have solved this many times over. Therefore, you will naturally know more about what the customer is facing, and you have important realities to share about how these other companies were wrong, how they failed, and how the customer is about to make the same mistake. With your guidance, the customer will have an opportunity to avoid the same pitfalls by rethinking what constitutes an ideal solution.

Create tension by challenging the customer's views with disruptive insight. You will need to be comfortable with creating this discomfort. You cannot be afraid or reluctant to challenge the customer in this polite, measured way. Customers will find value if you bring them new ideas that help them see things in a new way.

An elegant way to challenge the customer to think differently is to emphasize the importance of certain elements of your proposed solution. Provide this insight and challenge to the customer by making him or her think differently. Say, for example:

"Four out of five companies with this same thinking encountered problems in the first year after going with a cheaper, slower product. One company, for example, didn't anticipate having problems with their approach, and it caused them to miss important goals. After six to nine months, they called us back in for help. Besides losing time and wasting money, our contacts were embarrassed within their organization, having made the cheap decision without considering the long-term realities. Since you are similar to these organizations I've described, consider that the chances are likely for a similar predicament happening to you as well. It is becoming clear that you will be at risk in the same ways if you don't reconsider. What are the ramifications of having made this call in a year? We recommend that you reconsider your ideal solution to avoid this. Can you do that?"

Ideally, someone outside of sales needs to provide these failure case studies. Marketing can often provide support by doing a study on customers who switch from competitors. If marketing doesn't have it, salespeople can use data based on their own experience and frame it by saying, "Based on my experience over the past three years working with companies like yours, I have seen four out of five companies come back to me because of these problems."

A Few More Words on Challenging Customers

As I've emphasized throughout this book, it's important to note that excelling in sales does not always mean focusing on closing the deal. Before you can close, you've got to have a strong connection with the customer. You have to be tuned in to customers' mind-sets in order to challenge them. If you challenge a customer at the wrong time, it can backfire. If you challenge a customer at the right time, you show that you are in alignment and have a connection—and that will determine your success in building your personal value currency and ultimately making the sale.

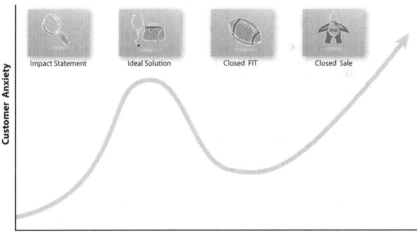

Here's a rule of thumb to follow: When customer anxiety is low, like when they are feeling they are doing just fine or they have the better solution than yours, it's time to challenge them. If the customer's anxiety is high, like when you first meet them or they are trying to make a decision, it's time to calm them. It takes some time to learn how to align with people's anxiety levels, but by understanding the four faces approach, it becomes second nature.

You will be challenging customers during the sleuth face, when they think they are doing just fine. This is the time to hit them with your provocative impact statement that sheds light on an emerging problem.

In the doctor face of the sales process, anxiety is going to be higher, as customers observe your behavior on your initial meeting. Therefore, it's not the best time to go in with guns blazing, telling customers they are wrong and challenging them. It's just like when you go into a doctor's office, and tension is high. Should your doctor be challenging you now? You know you need help, and that is why you are there in the office asking for an answer. Imagine walking into the office and having the doctor try to show how smart he or she is by saying, "I read that one out of five people suffer a stroke at age sixty?" What a piece of self-aggrandizing data, which may or may not pertain to you at all. It might actually be meaningless trivia to you. You might not like that feeble attempt of trying to be a show-off very much, but if the doctor calmed you down first, you might be more receptive to what he or she had to say.

When you go to see a doctor, you are already interested in learning more about how the doctor can help you. You know you need help, but you don't know what the answer is. That is why you are there in the doctor's office! You want answers, not provocative statements to get you interested in medical help.

Similarly, when you are in the doctor face of sales, customers are already interested in meeting you. They are looking for a solution to a problem, and thanks to your impact statement, they feel challenged already. Now they are interested in spending time with you, watching closely to see whether you can listen, empathize, and relate to their situation. This is not the time to challenge them again on why they should be meeting you. Instead, stick with their initial willingness to meet and build on it. You will challenge them again in the next face; the opening of your initial doctor meetings is not the time to do it. If you make the mistake of getting the "when" wrong and start prematurely rattling off challenges, you'll turn the conversation away from what customers are there to talk about—their situation—and you'll reduce your personal value currency by coming across as overaggressive at this early stage.

At a recent sales training event I participated in, I was invited to role-play as the salesperson having an initial doctor meeting about a customer's business situation. I knew the customer was interested in my help and therefore had invested time for the appointment. The trainers were jumping up and down, telling me to walk in with a "Did you know" statement instead of seeking to understand the customer's situation. How uncomfortable for any customer to have to endure that! Patients would not endure a doctor who treated them in this manner. Don't be overzealous and challenge customers on your first doctor meeting; this will just raise their defenses. Instead, be a doctor, and then you can challenge them like crazy as the quarterback.

During the quarterback face of the sales process, customers are optimistically looking forward to your presentation and their anxiety is lower. This is an ideal time to challenge the customer to think different and politely make your argument.

The quarterback face of sales is the ideal time to gently challenge the customer's thoughts and get the thinking going in new directions.

In the hero face of the sales process that we'll discuss in part 4, the anxiety will be highest. Customers will be wondering if they should do what you suggest and make a decision. When you are about to take a chance, do you need people telling you about the risks of doing it? No, you already know the risks. You need people to support you as you weigh the risks and make a decision one way or the other. You are looking for support, not a challenge. Don't challenge the customer in the hero face of sales.

CHAPTER 14

Call the Next Play

AFTER ALL YOUR quarterback efforts to make your presentation and challenge customers to see your solution as the best fit, you have to know one thing: Did your score? In other words, did your presentation on your proposed solution win the customer over? Will it be a thumbs-up or thumbs-down from each stakeholder? You have earned the right to know, since you drove the ball all the way down the field and made your best attempt. You did all that work, and now you deserve to know whether you scored a good fit or not. It's time to politely insist on hearing the answer to this question, even if you have to put on your helmet and brace for bad news. Approach each decision stakeholder for an answer with questions like these:

- "Are all the people involved with this decision convinced that this solution fits with your vision of your ideal solution?"
- "Are there others involved in this decision who must answer this question as well?"

At this point, the votes from stakeholders will be in, and you'll know if you still face resistance or not. Tally up all the stakeholder votes to determine your next play. Ask your champion for support with your selected plays. There are three to choose from.

Play 1: Hurry-Up Offense

When all stakeholders agree that your proposed solution is a good fit, advance to the hero face in a hurry-up offensive play. Once you have agreed on a solution fit with all stakeholders, close this face and advance this opportunity to the face of the hero to close the sale. This advance action will be a positive for customers, since you will take control of the next action step without pushing them. Explain the step ahead and guide or "pull" your customer along by saying, "Based on our confirmed fit, our next step will be to meet to discuss terms to finalize an agreement."

Use this play to move quickly to increase the tempo, present your full proposal, and close the sale. You'll leave the face of the quarterback and ask your champion to set a meeting in order to finalize an agreement in the face of the hero.

Play 2: "Trojan Horse" Trick Play

Sometimes, stakeholders vote unanimously that one small part of your proposed solution is a good fit, but they are not convinced about the majority of your solution. They are engaged and focused on one specific aspect of your solution and seem to dwell on that topic by asking the same types of questions repeatedly.

When all of the stakeholders agree that only a small part of your solution is a good fit, it's time to call the "Trojan horse" trick play as your next step. The Greeks invented the Trojan horse strategy during the Trojan War, constructing a huge wooden horse to hide a select force of men inside. When the Greeks pretended to sail away, the Trojans pulled the horse into their city as a victory trophy. That night, the Greek force crept out of the horse, opened the gates for the rest of the Greek army, and destroyed the city of Troy, decisively winning the war.

This trick play counts on subterfuge. You will take the small piece of your solution the stakeholders are in agreement with as a fit and redefine the scope of your proposal to be more narrow. Advance this newly defined opportunity to the next face to close the sale as the hero. Once this piece is closed, you can expand your solution to grow from within the customer's organization.

Play 3: Power Play

When all the stakeholders except your decision maker agree your proposed solution is a good fit, you must stay with the quarterback face and call a power play. In this case, your decision maker will likely seem distant and fail to engage with you.

If your decision maker is holding you back while everyone else is voting for you, this power play calls for you to identify and engage new, influential executives to exert pressure on the decision maker. These higher-level executives have not been involved but will care about the outcome. Perhaps they are the decision maker's internal peers or colleagues in different business units. Identify these power-play stakeholders specifically because they will find value in aspects of your solution. Ask your champion to set a meeting with these executives to provide a briefing for your presentation, drawing attention to those elements that will impact them.

To implement this play, leverage your champion. Ask him or her to identify these new power-play executives by saying, "We need to alert the executives who will be negatively impacted if we don't proceed. Who are the decision maker's internal peers who will feel these ramifications? Can you arrange a meeting with them?"

Scenarios & Appropriate Plays:

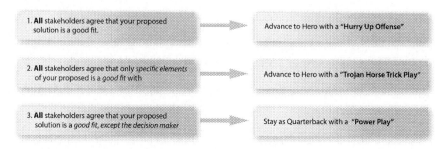

1. **All** stakeholders agree that your proposed solution is a good fit.

   Advance to Hero with a **"Hurry Up Offense"**

2. **All** stakeholders agree that only *specific elements* of your proposed is a *good fit* with

   Advance to Hero with a **"Trojan Horse Trick Play"**

3. **All** stakeholders agree that your proposed solution is a *good fit, except the decision maker*

   Stay as Quarterback with a **"Power Play"**

CHAPTER 15

Recap of the Quarterback Approach

LET'S RECAP THE key points regarding the quarterback stage of the Four Faces of Sales.

- Present your ideal solution while making sure to start with the customer's own vision of a way to address an issue or problem.
- Sell on your people, your company, and your service or product.
- Tactfully challenge your customer to find better ways of solving an existing problem.
- Use the Feel-Felt-Found sales tactic to challenge the customer's ideal solution.
- Assess the customer's risk tolerance for a lower priced solution.

The quarterback in sales gets things done. The key objective is to get customers fully engaged in addressing their problem and encouraging an in-depth discussion while presenting your solution. Now is the time to prove that your service or product is the best solution for the customer. When you feel the customer agrees to a good fit, move in for the close in the next face.

Part 4

The Hero Face

When you ask for the sale, be a hero.

CHAPTER 16

The Hero Closer

CUSTOMERS FEEL PRESSURED when you ask for the sale before they are ready to buy. The hero knows when the customer is ready and how to take control in a calming way to finalize an agreement. In the story about "Julie's Dilemma" at the start of this book, Julie and I reminded Bob Glaser and his executive team about our journey together, and from then on they were able to confidently conclude we were the best solution. You can do that just as effectively.

Learning from Julie

"They're out," Julie announced in frustration. "They've got cold feet; the deal is dead." Once again, Julie had high expectations to close a sale and ended up empty-handed. Her disappointment and confusion were certainly understandable. As in the past, the meeting had started off well, with everyone seemingly on the same page. As it unfolded, however, the customer's attitude changed, and the customer began backing away from making a commitment. Issues seemed to surface out of the blue until finally the customer bowed out, leaving Julie feeling blindsided.

How do these surprise failures happen when success seems certain? You should be able to guess by now—the "when" elements were contributing to Julie's eleventh-hour losses. Even though she knew what action to take—asking for the sale—I came to realize that Julie's lack of success occurred when she got the "when" wrong.

"When": Too Slow to Close

Sometimes Julie moved too cautiously when finalizing the sale. Happy that she was finally at the proposal stage, Julie worried about making a mistake and scaring the customer away. She avoided calling customers and waited patiently for them to respond, her goal being to give customers room and time to make a decision without pressure. This approach backfired, however, because it made her appear tentative just when the customer was looking to her for strength and support.

When Julie just sent along the proposal without asking to meet to discuss customers' comfort level, again trying not to be pushy, this opened the door to more doubt. The already jittery customers interpreted her politeness as a sign of inexperience and disorganization, which left them feeling alone and exposed. Despite her good intentions, Julie had inadvertently iced the customer out.

"When": Too Fast to Close

At other times, Julie was overzealous and attempted to close the sale too quickly. She resorted to asking for the order early and often. However, while Julie employed this technique in an attempt to get feedback and overcome any objections, she instead raised her customers' stress level. Julie was badgering customers with her repeated, though polite, requests to finalize the sales at a time when what the customers really needed from her was support.

While Julie thought she was doing the right thing by asking for the sale, she unknowingly became a high-pressure salesperson in her customers' eyes. Julie inadvertently gave up a lot of her personal value currency.

"You need to get close to the customer and become a calming and reassuring force now," I told Julie. Then everything changed for the better.

Being a hero is really easy once you get the hang of it, reducing your customer's anxiety levels at a critical point and finally landing the sale.

The hero face of sales does not require a heavy-handed approach. In fact, the last thing you want to do is pressure customers at this stage of the game. You could blow all that hard work you put into the process, and you could lose every last cent of your all-important personal value currency. Instead, the approach demands an awareness of where customers are coming from.

The Sales Hero to the Rescue

Making important decisions is stressful. Realize that customers may be worried and having second thoughts. Concerns and doubts will start swirling around in their heads. Their selection will expose them to judgment from peers and management, and any misstep will be costly to the organization and to them personally. They're under a great deal of pressure—externally and self-imposed—to make the right choice.

They may be thinking, *I hope going with you is the right decision. I'll have to trust that you will deliver on what you've promised and will be supportive and responsive if something goes wrong.*

With high anxiety levels at this point, spend your personal value currency to calm the customer down. It is to your advantage after all the patience and discipline you have practiced with the customer to solely focus on solving the problem, not pushing product. Your approach felt good to the customer, and he or she now trusts you immensely—this is your personal value currency. Now you have true power to flex since you followed the Four Faces of Sales.

During this period of high anxiety, the customer tends to look for strength and direction from a trusted source in order to make the right decision. To help the customer deal with any apprehension, you need to be that trusted source of strength and direction, instilling confidence so the customer will finalize the sale.

Your personal value currency will help you close the sale when the customer is anxious about making a buying decision.

Now is the time to "cash in" your personal value currency accumulated as the result of all your past sales interactions as the sleuth, doctor, and quarterback. During each face interaction, you made small deposits into the personal value currency bank because of the positive, branded experiences the customer had. Now, your ability to influence the customer directly correlates to the amount of personal value currency you have in the bank.

If you have amassed personal value currency during your past interactions, the bank will be full and you'll be ready to make a withdrawal and influence your customer. The customer will trust you when you say:

> "You are right, this is a big decision. But we have worked together for the last three months to analyze your need and solve your problem. Yes, it is a big decision, but accepting my proposal is the right thing to do."

Never will you be in a stronger position to close the sale than when you have personal value currency to cash in. Your new face, one that represents coolness under pressure, is the face of the hero. As the hero, you are the customer's trusted source of strength and direction during a time of stress.

How do heroes act during a time of panic, chaos, and pressure? Do they sit back quietly and hope things work out in their favor? No, of course not. They swoop into action and take care of things with confidence. The sales hero knows how to influence the customer and instill confidence in the buying decision. Heroes know how to encourage the customer to say yes to the proposal.

You don't have to be a superhero to get it done and done right, but you do have to go through the preceding steps of being a sleuth, doctor, and quarterback to get to this stage. Once you reach this point, you're almost home. Let's take a close look at how you can cross the finish line as a winner.

Your Personal Value Currency

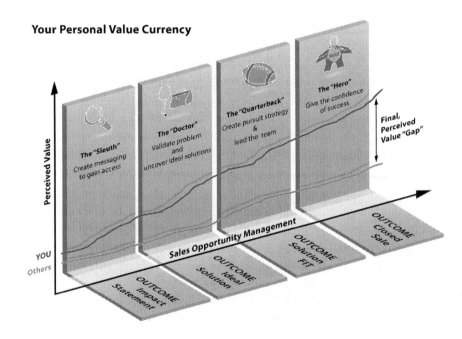

CHAPTER 17

The Final Approach

THE HERO CONFIDENTLY maintains control during the final approach by taking steps to build consensus and set a close meeting. This may sound easy enough, especially after you have worked so closely with the customer to arrive at this stage of the sales process. It's worth noting, though, that the majority of sales fall through in the final stages, when the customer must put his or her money on the line and make an important decision that will impact the company's profitability. It's natural for anxiety to run high and for people to want to back away. It's your job to give the customer every reason to move ahead.

A key element to a successful close is building consensus as the hero. Set up early surveillance, neutralize your opponents, and create a groundswell of support for your company's proposal, and good things will happen for you and your customer.

Early Surveillance

Since you have confirmed your solution is a good fit while wearing the face of the quarterback, you are close to finalizing a sale. However, you can easily be surprised and suddenly lose the sale. This is because the customer may have concerns, hesitations, and doubts that you don't know about.

To avoid these surprises, it is critical that you set up an early detection system with your champion that alerts you to any trouble brewing. To determine if everyone is on the same page, ask these questions:

- "What are the other decision stakeholders saying about our proposal?"
- "Are they all comfortable working with me and my company?"
- "How are we ranked versus alternative proposals?"
- "What do they like about other proposed solutions that we don't offer?"
- "Is there anything I should know that might prevent us from moving forward with an agreement?"

Neutralize Opponents

Once you have early surveillance in place, you must attack any trouble spots you find. Your surveillance may reveal a stakeholder who is against your proposed solution: this is your hidden opponent. You may never have met this individual during your previous interactions, or your opponent may have attended your meetings and conference calls but remained silent.

Such opponents can be against change of any kind for any number of reasons. They may see your proposed solution as an unnecessary change. These opponents believe that stability outweighs most improvement efforts and just want to keep the status quo. They may favor another solution over yours as a better fit for them. These opponents believe alternative solutions outrank yours as a better fit for their ideal solution in mind. Regardless, opponent stakeholders predisposed against you will choose to *not* engage with you or share any information. They do damage, however, by fighting against you behind the scenes, quietly influencing the organization in the hopes that your solution will be rejected.

If your surveillance discovers a hidden opponent, you must draw him or her out into the open. Do so with an incentive, offering something that this individual is attracted to or wants to hear more about. Offer an informational session or invite them to a group lunch with a theme that supports your opponent's fight against your solution—a meeting entitled "Discuss Pros/Cons of Options" or something to that effect. Your opponent will see this as an opportunity to gain support for his or her side and may even get excited enough to invite others to join in.

Now, when the meeting begins, your opponent will be out of hiding, and you can address his or her concerns directly and respectfully. Begin the meeting by providing case studies and proof of successes that refute the opponent's views. That's not what the opponent will want to hear, but it's fair game since it falls within the context of the meeting. Point out that there is low risk in accepting your solution and ask for feedback from around the room, leaving the opponent until last. Respectfully ask the opponent:

"I must have missed you during our meetings, and I value your thoughts on this. Can I better understand if you see risks stemming from the solution we are proposing?"

Your opponent's hiding days are over. He or she has been respectfully exposed with other stakeholders in the room. Will the opponent take a stand against everyone? When opponents can no longer hide and the power of their behind-the-scenes activity is taken away, they will most likely submit to and concede with the others. They will be neutralized.

Build Groundswell

To create a groundswell of support, groom your champion to become your "internal salesperson" who will facilitate conversations among the other stakeholders and create favorable office chatter. You will need to invest time and effort to coach and equip your champion to be successful. Provide assets your champion can use to influence his or her colleagues. Specifically, set champions up with all the tools you used as the salesperson earlier on, including relevant articles, new research data about trends, and brochures or websites that will reference new innovations.

Consider training your champion to become an expert on your product so he or she can present, demonstrate, and answer questions on your behalf internally. Have your trainers, consultants, or technical team spend time to instruct your champion on the inner workings of your product, making him or her more powerful and credible.

Once your champion is armed with these skills and information, ask him or her to approach fellow decision stakeholders and encourage them to accept your proposal. Coach your champion to start a domino effect by asking that each stakeholder share a favorable outlook with other stakeholders. Through the champion's efforts and actions, opinions can grow into a groundswell, with stakeholders talking together in favor of your solution.

CHAPTER 18

Finalizing the Agreement

YOUR NEXT STEP as the hero is to set a meeting to finalize the agreement. Ask your champion to arrange this meeting and ensure that the final decision maker will be present and understand that the purpose of the meeting is to finalize the sale. If this is difficult for the champion, spend your personal value currency to exert influence on the champion to make this happen. Say something like this:

> "The purpose of this meeting is to review our proposal, answer any questions, and finalize an agreement. Therefore, it is important to hear any questions from your decision maker in order to answer them properly and start the business relationship in the proper way. If you agree, will you make sure the decision maker is present?"

To start this meeting, think small. That is, focus the beginning of the conversation on achieving two small agreements. These small agreements are designed to build momentum toward signing the final agreement. These two agreements are the *comfort close* and the *timeline close*. Confirm each small agreement before moving ahead to the final close.

Comfort Close

Build a comfort level by reminding customers that your solution is the best fit to meet their vision of an ideal solution. As the quarterback, you helped customers come to see that your solution is a good fit for them—your fit agreement. This is your anchor now.

It's important that you leave no room for customers to cast doubt that your solution is a good fit. If they are uncomfortable and have concerns about your solution at this point, it can slow down or even derail your ability to close the sale. If customers question the fit of your solution at this meeting, don't let them take you backward. Instead, defend your position by reminding the customer about your journey.

Since you have already proven that your solution is a good fit, you do not need to continue reviewing this known fact. Point out that the fit agreement is an achievement that took a lot of hard work from both sides and that there's no looking back. You could say:

> "Remember we discussed this point during our presentations with your team? We worked it through and your team said that they were happy with our answer. We both invested time, energy, and creative thinking during demonstrations and presentations that are completed now. Therefore, we do not need to go back and review this again. Right? Are you comfortable to move forward now?"

Now, this assumes that you will get sincere answers to these questions. If you find that this becomes a pattern of recurring questions causing friction, recycling, and reminding of activities past, you might have a customer who will become a time drain on you. Consider that you want to work with profitable customers, and if these questions lead you to recognize a high-maintenance, time-consuming, low-profit customer, you always have the right to choose not to do business with that customer.

Naturally, it's best not to find out you've got a hassle on your hands when you're about to close the sale. Watch for warning signs from the doctor stage on. You don't want to bail at the first indication of trouble, but by all means keep in mind that wasted time costs you and your company money. Don't be afraid to recognize troublesome customers and reduce your efforts and expectations if they don't improve.

Timeline Close

Another way to move the closing process forward is to build a sense of urgency with customers by putting their timeline in the spotlight. Ask, "What date do you need your solution to be up and running and successfully working by?"

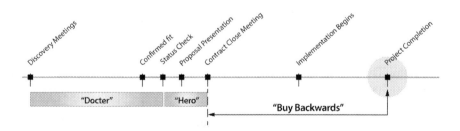

Use the customer's future completion date to motivate him or her to make a decision to meet that deadline. Place the timeline sheet in front of the customer. Starting at the completion date (on the right of the sheet), work backward (toward the left of the sheet) and highlight the actions necessary to meet the date. Let the timeline show when the customer needs to finalize the agreement in order to meet the desired deadline.

To create urgency without pressuring, simply let the timeline do the talking. Offer the customer assurance that you will get the solution up and running by the deadline if the agreement is signed now. Point out the risks of missed deadlines if the agreement is not finalized now. Say something like this:

> "I believe it is in your best interest that we finalize this agreement today in order to make your delivery goals. Let's work together to close it now so we do not miss your timeline."

Putting the customer's needs in front of yours serves the interests of both parties.

The party whose timeline is exposed has less power, so make sure it's the customer's timeline, not yours, that's on the table. Be certain not to reveal your own timeline; never give information regarding your monthly or quarterly quotas, because a smart negotiator will jump at the chance to use this to his or her benefit. You will now be in the weaker position, and knowing you'll have reported this deal as having a high probability of success to your sales management team, the customer will proceed to wear you down with last-minute ultimatums and concessions. Your timeline can and will be used against you, so keep quiet about it and turn the timeline spotlight on the customer.

CHAPTER 19

Going for the Gold

IN THE FINAL analysis, you're the one who will close the sale. You've got to have the willpower to move forward to the final stage. In short, you have to be a real hero in the sales arena. When you've gone through all the different faces of sales and you've reached this point, it's time to come right out and ask for the deal. In a confident, calm manner, sit or stand next to your customer and turn his or her attention to the proposal. Explain each line item and ask to finalize the agreement. Here's an example of what you could say:

> "Now, in order for us to get to work, let's finalize this agreement. Can you confirm we have an agreement?"

If the decision maker does not actually sign the agreement, he or she will pass it to the internal procurement department to review the commercial terms and have another executive (usually in finance) sign it. If the decision maker will be signing the agreement, put a small "x" where the proposal is to be signed, hand the customer your pen, and say, "Please sign here."

Don't blink. After you ask the decision maker to sign, remain silent. When the decision maker stops and looks at you as though it's time for you to talk, just sit there and do not say a word. This is a staring contest now, and whoever can remain silent and not blink (with a smile) wins. If anyone asks a question, answer it, and make the same request again. Stay on course and repeat this process while staying silent until the customer complies.

Overcoming Price Objections

Obviously, you should all be clear on the price at this point, but sometimes even the best customers can throw a monkey wrench into the works when the deal is about to go through. The most common monkey wrench is price. Customers may question the price simply out of principle. Others might have received pressure from top management, or even the board of directors, and they'll be asking for a price reduction because the deal won't go through without one.

For example, you might get a customer who will say, "Your price seems too high," and then sit back to watch the salespeople squirm and scramble to save the sale. However, you need not be afraid of this tactic. Respond directly, by telling the customer that price integrity and transparency are core values of your company. In fairness, your company offers full transparency of price for all customers. Say something like this:

> "We are fully transparent on our price for all of our customers in order to be fair and maintain the highest level of integrity. It is difficult to justify the fairness of having you pay a lower price and receive the same services as other customers."

If that doesn't work (it probably won't), take these three actions to counter their price request.

Ask the Customer to Make an Offer

Since you made the first offer in your proposal, it's the customer's turn now. Do not react to the challenge by rambling that your proposal has competitive prices and so on. Don't negotiate by immediately jumping into the discussion with a lower price. That's negotiating with yourself and signals weakness and desperation, and may even cause the customer to be skeptical that your price is even legitimate.

Instead, answer them with your own questions. Ask customers why they believe the price is too high, and put the burden on them to justify that claim. Get them talking, but stay right on point. Say something like this:

> "I am unclear what you mean when you say the price looks high. Can you explain? What are you comparing us to when you say the price is too high? Why do you believe the price is too high? What do you feel the price should be?"

Ask the Customer to Explain the Offer

Don't get caught up in arguing over what the customer wants, because it tends to lock the two of you against each other. The downside of this tactic is that the more customers clarify their position and defend it, the more committed they become to winning. When the other side's ego becomes associated with a position, they dig in to save face rather than reconcile and come to an agreement. To avoid this situation, use your personal value currency to keep things civil and moving forward. Get the customer to justify that request for a price reduction by focusing on their underlying interests—*why* they made their request. Ask, "May I ask how you arrived at this number?" When they answer this, maintain a neutral expression and write it down. Keep a poker face.

If you find yourself in the midst of a price negotiation at this stage and it hits a brick wall, you'll have to be ready to pull out of the deal. The good news is that most excellent salespeople, people like yourself, are able to salvage the majority of deals that threaten to go south on them at the last minute. One effective way to go is to ask customers what they are willing to do without.

Ask If the Customer Is Willing to Accept the Risks

In the mechanics of lowering the price, explain that you will need to remove something from the proposal in return. It's not in the customer's best interest to cut corners. Make sure you say that. Then, if the customer insists on a lower price, ask what risk level he or she is willing to accept in order to lower price. Remind customers about the conversations on risk vs. price balance (see chapter 12). Illustrate the laws of balance for them again.

Here's a sample script for reminding the customer of this point:

> "Remember we discussed the failure rates of companies that rebalance their price/risk model to a lower price with a lesser performing product? As you may recall, four out of five of these companies called us back after six to nine months and wasted precious time and money and personal reputation.

We recommend that you reconsider the importance
of price over risk. Are you really willing to take on
increased risk for a lower price?"

As they ponder this, point out that the price they pay will become
irrelevant over time. However, they will remember if they fail or
have problems with a cheaper option. You could say:

"In a year from now, the price will be forgotten. But
the lower price without our company, people, and
product will be remembered for years to come."

After taking these three actions, you may or may not be able to
meet the customer's new price request. Whatever you do in terms
of giving a price concession, let your customers think they won.
When they give in, allow them to keep their dignity. This is not
about beating your opponent into submission. Remember, the side
that loses in the negotiation will find ways to make the other pay for
this loss after the contract is finalized. If you aggravate customers and
force them into unfavorable agreements, they will resent you for it
and bring more confrontation into the ongoing relationship, if there
is one. Instead, help the customer save face. Say something like this:

"You are a fair negotiator, and I know we can agree on
the smartest proposal for your success at the best price.
I am sure you understand that it would be prohibitive
to make price concessions without exposing ourselves
to risks and issues. Therefore, I believe we can agree
on the right decision to keep this a mutually beneficial
agreement."

After customers agree and sign the contract, stand up, shake hands, smile, and give a compliment:

"Congratulations, we have an agreement. Well played. We look forward to getting to work on this important initiative. We are sure our initiative will yield solid results. Thank you for the opportunity to be of service."

CHAPTER 20

Recap of the Hero Approach

LET'S REVIEW WHAT we learned about the hero face of sales.

- Now is the time to spend your personal value currency to close the sale.
- Don't challenge the customer at this stage. Instead, offer all the support you can to lessen the anxiety about the buying decision.
- Detect and neutralize opposition to the sale as early as possible.
- Use your champion contact to create a groundswell of support for your proposal.
- Use the Comfort and Timeline Closing approach during your close meeting.
- Overcome last-minute objections regarding price.

Using the Four Faces of Sales process, you will pull ahead of the competition and gain that critical edge that will propel you to the next level in your career. Closing a sale gives you a terrific feeling deep down in your bones. If you're a real pro, the close also gives you a rush and a sense of pride in a job well done.

Of course, the sales business is all about the money, but as I've been saying throughout the book, selling is about much more than that. It's about helping other people connect with a service or product they need to improve their situation. It's about solving problems. It's about reaching out and touching the lives of your customers and making them better.

As you go about implementing the approach in this book, bear in mind that the Four Faces of Sales represents a new and exciting way of selling. With information and knowledge comes power, and with power comes influence. The ability to identify and harness the power of the Four Faces of Sales will translate into increased sales and more profit for you and your company. You are now on your way to a more rewarding career in sales.

Conclusion

USING THE FOUR Faces of Sales process, you will know when to take action. As you have read, this selling process is carefully orchestrated. Each face represents a specific objective that must be accomplished in alignment with the customer's thinking. When you have achieved that objective, you must phase out of—or close—that face and move on to the next one. Progressing through each face is what takes the salesperson and the customer through to the final sale.

It's all about "when." The goal of the Four Faces of Sales process is to build your personal value currency. Understanding how to get the "when" actions right will enable you to achieve each face's objective—which, in turn, will bring you to this goal.

The faces have names that help you clearly distinguish between the different thought processes and behaviors required in each phase. As the captain of this process, you must know when to move from one face to the next in response to your customer. As a result, you will create a positive branded buying experience that feels good to the customer—and to you. You'll differentiate yourself from the competition and increase your personal value currency while truly helping your customers solve their problems.

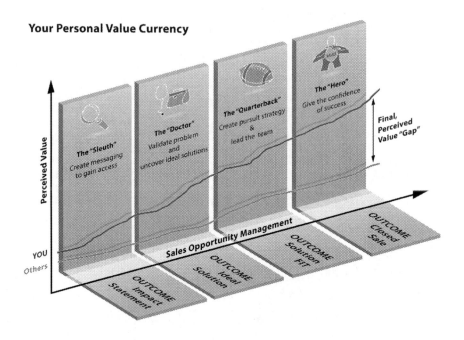

Your Personal Value Currency

It's All about You Now!

Today's customers are seeking value, and they judge that value based on how you interact with them, not just on what you sell. More than ever, creating a branded experience for the customer while he or she works with you is critical to sales success. There's no way around this: customers' buying decisions are influenced by their conversations and interactions with you.

Just think about that. Sales are driven by the experience the customer has with you—not your company, not your product, but *you*. The customer's experience has more influence than anything else, so every interaction with your customer has greater weight than ever before. That weight is on your shoulders. All eyes are on you!

You've now learned the Four Faces of Sales process. The entire process is centered on the idea that the customer's branded experience is better when you stay in alignment with the way the customer buys. When she used the Four Faces process, Julie's personal value currency skyrocketed and she was off to the races. You can be too.